The Irwin Series in Management and the Behavioral Sciences

L. L. Cummings and *E. Kirby Warren*   Consulting Editors

John F. Mee   Advisory Editor

General Management

An Analytical Approach

Norman A. Berg

Graduate School of Business Administration
Harvard University

1984

RICHARD D. IRWIN, INC.   Homewood, Illinois   60430

© RICHARD D. IRWIN, INC., 1984

85-4394

ISBN 0-256-02910-5

Library of Congress Catalog Card No. 83–82964

Printed in the United States of America

1 2 3 4 5 6 7 8 9 0 ML 1 0 9 8 7 6 5 4

For Cynthia

PREFACE

$\mathbf{T}$his is a book about the process of General Management. It is a substantial modification of the text portion of the eighth edition of *Policy Formulation and Administration*,[1] a book of text and cases used in courses dealing with the job of the general manager. The book is designed to help you increase your understanding of the requirements of that job and to help you develop your skills in the application of an analytical process that is useful in the performance of that job. The text addresses the task of general management in the diversified firm as well as the job of the general manager in the single-business firm.

The book is intended for three audiences:

1. The student of business administration in a college or university who is enrolled in courses in the broad area of Management, and especially Business Policy.

2. The executive who is a participant in an executive development program which includes attention to the job of the general manager.

3. The practicing executive who is attempting on his own to improve his/her* skills as a general manager.

The book is intended primarily for readers with some background in business administration—achieved in the classroom,

---

[1]All footnotes are shown in Appendix B.

*Throughout the text masculine pronouns alone will sometimes be used instead of the more accurate dual form because of simplicity of presentation.

through experience, or (preferably) both. It is designed to be used in conjunction with cases chosen by the instructor either from the large number of individual cases available [2] or from published casebooks. It should be especially useful in conjunction with management development seminars or courses for executives as a brief, practice-oriented text dealing with the job of the general manager.

The usefulness of the book is not limited to those who already are, or are soon to become, general managers. Although most will assume that role only after years of gaining experience in a functional field or a staff capacity, all those who plan to work in any purposive organization can benefit greatly from an exposure to the problems and responsibilities of the general manager, distant though they may be. An understanding of the broader framework into which your contributions must fit can only serve to improve the quality of those contributions. Such an understanding will also be of benefit, for the same reasons, to those who ultimately may become management consultants or financial advisors to the corporation.

The knowledge, skills, and attitudes required of the successful general manager are not gained overnight. An early exposure to the nature of the job is beneficial in enabling you to seek and to learn from experiences which will increase your chances of becoming a general manager and improve your performance once you are one.

Although the terminology of the book and the experiences on which it is based derive primarily from business organizations, the critical tasks of the manager in any purposive organization have much in common with those of the business practitioner. The problems of formulating and implementing strategy in the purposive or administrative unit are sufficiently similar so that the analytical approach suggested should be useful in those settings as well.

Characteristics

The purposes of the book and the audience for which it is intended have influenced its characteristics in a number of ways:

1. The book is concerned with the *process* by which the general manager (or president or division manager) of a business deals with the *totality* of his job and his responsibilities. It does not dwell greatly on a listing of responsibilities, a description of daily activities, an explanation of the principles of management, or an elaboration of specialized analytical techniques. Neither is it a collection of readings, although readings are suggested. The emphasis is on understanding the nature of the general manager's job in its totality and on developing an approach useful in solving the problems encountered in that job.

2. The approach suggested is a relatively simple conceptual scheme which is easy to state but requires work, experience, and judgment to apply to the specific situation. The attempt is to simplify the complex, not provide complicated models that are unlikely to be used or, if used, applied mechanistically. One should not equate *complex* with *advanced* or *superior.*

3. The approach stems from the observation of business practice and is intended to meet the needs of practitioners. It has been developed over time by faculty of the Harvard Business School, as described more fully in the next section, and is based on their research and consulting activities and the development and teaching of a large number of cases describing actual business situations. It is not a theory derived from economic or legal models of the firm, but it is normative to the extent that it prescribes an approach for the practitioner to follow in developing the solutions to his problems as he sees them.

4. Because the approach is practitioner-oriented and deals with a managerial process, there is a strong emphasis on developing what is called "The Administrative Point of View." The test of analyses and recommendations will be whether they address the problems of the general manager in the specific situation in a sensible way. The role adopted throughout will be that of the involved manager dealing with actual problems, not the observer or the scholar dealing with simplified or generalized problems.

Plan of the Book

The book is organized into three parts. Part 1, The Job of the General Manager, elaborates on some of the points raised in the Preface and develops further the nature and importance of the job of the general manager. The use of the case method from the viewpoint of the student and the role of readings (listed in Appendix A) are also discussed.

Part 2, The Single-Business Company, is devoted to the development of an approach to the job of the general manager in the single-business company. This format was chosen because the concepts needed, though applicable to the diversified corporation as described in Part 3, have been developed and can best be learned by examining situations involving a single product and market and a single functional organization.

In Part 2, Chapter 2 develops the concept of strategy: its purposes and content. Chapter 3 breaks down the job of the general manager into the broad areas of formulation and implementation of strategy, interrelated in practice but separable for analytical purposes. An analytical model is described which specifies that the principal factors the manager should take into account in the formulation of strategy are the environment (Chapter 4), the corporate resources (Chapter 5), the values of management (Chapter 6), and the broader responsibilities of the corporation (Chapter 7). Evaluated in relation to each other, these are the major elements entering into the strategy formulation process.

Chapter 8 describes, in a similar manner, an approach to the implementation of corporate strategy or the task of gaining the commitment of the organization to the accomplishment of the strategy. The demands on the organization stem from the requirements of the strategy, and the ability of an organization to meet the demands placed upon it must be taken into account in the formulation of the strategy. The principal elements that the manager has to work with, or his sources of influence, are the organization structure, the information system, the pattern of rewards in terms of pay and promotion, the allocation of resources, and his own leadership role and abilities. Chapter 9 deals with the manager as a leader. It is these elements, once again considered in relation to each other, that determine the effectiveness of the organizational efforts in achieving the broader objectives of the firm.

The general management tasks at the corporate level of the diversified firm, the most important form of industrial organization in this country in terms of sales, assets, and employment, are the subject of Part 3. Chapter 10 provides some background on the emergence of and the economic issues raised by the diversified firm, a topic deemed unnecessary to cover for the more familiar and less complex single-business firm. Chapter 11 describes how the complexities caused by multiple products and levels of management affect the task of formulating and implementing strategy in the diversified firm; and Chapter 12 develops further the concept of strategy as developed for the single-business firm to make it applicable to the diversified firm. Chapter 13 extends the framework of analysis as developed earlier to the management problems of the diversified firm; and Chapter 14 focuses on resource allocation problems and the usefulness of portfolio planning models. Chapter 15 describes various approaches to the role of the corporate office in the management of the diversified firm, an important and complex extension of the centralization-decentralization issue raised in earlier chapters.

The quantitative analytical techniques available, the data needed to make use of them, and the computational power needed to combine the two have all increased greatly in the last few decades. So has our ability to provide information promptly in almost any detail and combination to all levels of the organization. Management still requires a substantial amount of judgment and skill, however, even though many of the decisions that formerly could not be handled in a rigorous manner are now subject to analysis and solution by specialists. In contrast to the highly focused materials that are available to help you learn accounting conventions or the techniques of discounted cash flow analysis, there is no one book or technique that will enable you to learn the job of the general manager. That is both the challenge and the fascination of the field, which we hope you will share with us as you seek to develop your own abilities.

ACKNOWLEDGEMENTS

The analytical approach to the job of the general manager as described in this book is largely the product of my involvement in the Business Policy course at the Harvard Business School over the past two decades. I have also learned a great deal about general management in practice from my involvement in case and project research, consulting, directorships, and the teaching of executives. Although the individuals both inside and outside the school that have contributed to my ideas and to the development of the Business Policy course and this text are far too numerous to mention by name, two colleagues deserve special mention for their contributions over the years.

Professor C. Roland Christensen has contributed greatly to our understanding of the art of teaching by the case method, as well as to the development of teaching materials that convey the administrative complexity of the job of the general manager in a way that enables the student to learn and grow, not just memorize and recite. Professor Kenneth Andrews, another long-time colleague, has been equally skilled at providing intellectual stimulation, contributing to the development of the concepts, and articulating them in a highly persuasive way. Together, they have played a major role in helping those of us who have been their colleagues to strike a balance between detailed checklists and elegant but abstract models, and to make the teaching of general management relevant to practice without lapsing into simply reporting on practice. The earliest exposition of these still-evolving ideas was by Professor Andrews in 1963,[3] and the framework presented at that time has influenced greatly the considerable attention that has been devoted to the concept of strategy and the role of the general manager since then.

Little of this activity would have been possible, of course, were it not for the institutional environment at the Harvard Business School that encouraged and facilitated in innumerable ways the study and teaching of the job of the general manager in its totality.

For that support and encouragement, relatively rare in the academic world, I am highly grateful to our current Dean, John H. McArthur, and to his predecessors during this period, Deans Lawrence E. Fouraker and George P. Baker.

Norman A. Berg

CONTENTS

PART *1*

The Job of the General Manager

CHAPTER 1

The Job of the General Manager

The general manager of an organization is the person primarily responsible for the performance of that unit. In smaller companies and in single-business companies, the president is likely to be the only general manager. In large business organizations many positions are of a general management nature. These include the chief executive officer, or CEO, who may be either the chairman or the president; the chief operating officer, or COO, in the event that is a separate position; executive vice presidents and group vice presidents who have responsibility for business units; and division presidents or managers.

Although precise definitions neither exist nor are necessary, usually any person who has responsibility for the results of the overall activity and substantial control over the organizational inputs needed to provide the product or service is considered a general manager, as is any person to whom a general manager reports. Profit center managers who have reasonable control over the factors affecting their profits are general managers; cost center managers are not. The single-business company will often have only one true general manager; the multi-business company will have at least two and, in companies as large and diverse as Westinghouse and General Electric, possibly as many as five or six levels of general management and hundreds of general managers with various titles.

General management positions exist in service organizations as well as in manufacturing organizations, and in government and education as well as in the traditional private sector. The critical characteristics of the position are a responsibility for the overall

performance of the organization and reasonable control over the inputs needed to provide the product or service. There are few organizations in which some such position, regardless of the title given
the incumbent, does not exist. Professional service organizations,
such as law firms and accounting firms, and in some cases investment banking concerns, have been the most reluctant to bestow on
any one of their members the formal responsibility and authority of
a general manager. Such reluctance seems to stem from an emphasis
on a collegial rather than a hierarchical form of organization and
from personal preferences for the practice of their profession rather
than the practice of management. In the vast majority of institutions
organized to provide a product or service, however, whether public
or private, there will be a person or persons with the responsibilities
of a general manager.

It should be apparent that the responsibilities of the general manager are broad and numerous, the tasks often difficult, and the skills
required varied indeed. The rewards are large, however, in terms of
the satisfaction of being able to "run your own show," the outside
status and prestige our society confers on a successful manager, and
the monetary rewards that generally follow. It is a role in which few
students of business administration have had direct experience, one
to which many aspire, and one which often takes many years to reach.
For most, the route to general management will be through a progression of responsibilities in a functional area with perhaps some time
in staff positions. In most cases, the knowledge and skills required to
excel in a functional or staff capacity provide little direct training for
the challenges of the general management position.

RESPONSIBILITIES TO CONSTITUENCIES

When, as happens in many companies, there are multiple levels of
general management, managers at different levels will not have the
same responsibilities, authority, or knowledge. The nature of these
differences and the manner in which they are reconciled to form an
integrated whole are discussed in Part 3 of the book, which deals with
an analytical approach to general management in the diversified company. In any company, however, the general manager who is at the
apex of the organizational pyramid has a whole set of responsibilities
to external constituencies as well as his own organization.

Often referred to as the stakeholders in an enterprise, these constituencies include such claimants on the corporation and its resources as employees, shareholders, creditors, the local community,
and interest groups of various kinds. Employees have become much
more vocal and organized in their demands for participation in decisions affecting their future, and they increasingly reject the notion

that a company and its people can be bought, sold, or otherwise disposed of at the sole discretion of the current shareholders of the company. Shareholders, who have become more militant at what they see as a usurpation of their rights as owners by some professional managements, strive for a more direct voice in major corporate decisions. Other groups may express strong interests in such issues as plant location decisions, employment policies, whether the company is polluting the environment, product characteristics, or responsible advertising. Many seek contributions of corporate funds, executive time, or other resources for causes they consider worthy.

Strongly influencing the manner in which business is conducted and issues like the above are resolved are the laws, regulations, and regulatory bodies governing the conduct of business, all of which have increased greatly in the last few decades. Although the common stockholders are the legal owners of the business, very seldom do they exercise a direct voice in any of the above matters. The reconciliation of all of the demands on the corporation is the responsibility of the management with the input and oversight of the board of directors. The only certainty is that there is no way all of the claimants can be completely satisfied.

It would be more accurate to think of the president of a company, then, as having one pyramid below him—the company—but an inverted pyramid bearing down on him from above. He is at the apex of both, where all the pressures converge. Groups both inside and outside the company look to the president for the ultimate resolution of their claims and problems. And it is inherent in the job of the president that he must balance the conflicting demands of the many special interest groups in such a way that the long-run health of the enterprise is enhanced, and not just accede to short-run pressures or desires.

NATURE OF THE JOB

Many attempts have been made to describe in considerable detail the responsibilities of the general manager. We do not believe such checklists are particularly helpful in developing an analytical approach to meeting the totality of those responsibilities. Neither shall we attempt to describe in detail the daily activities of the general manager. Instead, we believe an observation by Professor C. R. Christensen, long a student of the roles, functions, and skills of the general manager, can tell us much about the nature of the job. He states that the good general manager needs the rare ability

> to lead effectively organizations whose complexities he can never fully understand, where his capacity to control directly the human

and physical forces comprising that organization is severely limited, and where he must make or review and assume ultimate responsibility for present decisions which commit concretely major resources for a fluid and unknown future.[1]

An approach to the primary responsibilities and task of the general manager which is consistent with the above brief description of its complexities and challenges has been well described by Andrews.[2] It is a conceptual scheme, not a listing of items or a set of principles, and it describes the three principal themes which have dominated the development of the Business Policy course at the Harvard Business School over the past several decades. The approach developed in this book, as does the Business Policy course at the Harvard Business School, will follow the same general breakdown. In Andrews' terminology, the activities of the general manager can be assigned to three roles: *organization leader, personal leader,* and *architect of corporate purpose.*

The meaning of these terms will become clearer as we proceed with the development of the approach to the job of the general manager. We will first deal with the *formulation* of corporate strategy, where the manager is the architect of corporate purpose. In the chapters dealing with the manager's role in the *implementation* of that purpose and the plans for achieving it, we see him acting as an organization leader. And in both of these activities, which are highly interrelated in practice, the *personal leadership skills* of the manager have a major impact on the outcome, a topic which is addressed frequently throughout the book but especially in Chapter 9.

CATEGORIES OF RESPONSIBILITY

Although a detailed list of the responsibilities of the general manager is neither essential for our purposes nor likely to be interesting in its own right, some elaboration beyond reponsibility for the broad tasks of formulation and implementation of strategy is useful.

1. The general manager is responsible for the establishment of long-term objectives for the company that are both challenging and attainable. He has to be sure that the problems and opportunities in the decades ahead receive sufficient thought and resources, and he has to have the vision to inspire others with what is desirable and may be possible. Visionaries can get both themselves and their organizations into trouble, as we all know, but that is no reason for ever replacing a visionary with a clerk.

2. The general manager is responsible for the development of supporting plans that will contribute to the accomplishment of the overall objectives selected. Strategies and plans for the functional areas have to be developed and coordinated, checkpoints which will test the feasibility of the strategies and plans have to be chosen, and contingent plans that can be adopted when things do not work out quite as planned must be available.

3. The general manager is responsible for the resolution of the inevitable conflicts that arise and trade-offs that must be made in many of the activities of the organization. Higher current profits can always be obtained at the expense of building for the future, and in the large corporation hundreds of decisions affecting that balance are made every day. Low-risk but low-potential-return projects will always compete with high-risk, high-potential-return projects for capital and management time. The research and development, manufacturing, marketing, finance, and personnel departments will always have issues in which the interests of one department are not in the interests of the others or of the corporation. Conflicts are unavoidable with regard to what outside groups may want the corporation to do and what the corporation can or wants to do. The manager cannot himself resolve every conflict that arises, but the system that resolves them is his responsibility.

4. The general manager is the leader of the organization and is responsible for the selection, development, motivation, and fair treatment of its members. The loyalty, dedication, and hard work that is characteristic of the members of so many of our successful organizations seldom occur in the absence of a manager who understands what elicits this kind of behavior and has the skills to bring it about.

5. Finally, the general manager is responsible for the overall performance of the organization. It is his responsibility to set and enforce the standards of performance necessary to achieve the objectives of the firm. It is his responsibility to see to it that the major activities of strategy formulation and implementation combine to create a strategy and a culture that lead to good performance. It is no defense to look at other examples of successful companies, whether they are Japanese or American, and say, "But it won't work here." His responsibility is to find something that *does* "work here."

It is unfortunately true more often than it should be that if the overall performance is good, the weaknesses in its achievement are little noticed, and if the performance is poor, what was done well is little rewarded. The only consolation a general manager has for possibly being held responsible for poor results that arise from factors beyond his control is that he may also receive credit for good results that may be equally due to factors beyond his control.

THE MANAGER'S ENVIRONMENT

It will be important for you to develop a sense of the atmosphere in which top-level executives work. Successful practicing managers are well aware of the nature and complexity of their environment. For others, the understanding has to come through reading, listening, and observing. The study of field-based cases dealing with problems of general managers is especially useful in this regard, as described later in this chapter. Mintzberg[3] and Kotter[4] have provided ample evidence to support the impressions of those who have had any contact with general managers that their days are made up of a myriad of activities, most of short duration, many part of a continuing process, and often arising in a seemingly random sequence. An appreciation of the need for a simple framework to lend order to the complexity of the general manager's job, as well as an understanding of how it can be applied, depends on some understanding of that job.

Managers work through and depend upon the skills and knowledge of other people; the higher you rise in an organization, the less you can perform the tasks required by yourself, drawing only on your own knowledge and skills. You will seldom have the luxury of working on one problem at a time for very long, however, or seeing one problem through to its solution at any one time. You are more likely to deal with a number of problems concurrently, each at a different stage of development, and some not proceeding in a logical straight line toward a solution. Indeed, many problems are not really "solved"; workable accommodations and compromises are developed that may serve for a time while other problems that have become more pressing are addressed.

The formulation and implementation of strategy is not likely to be as formal and logical a process in practice as it is described in most accounts of how managers "should" behave—and certainly not as well-ordered as problem-solving techniques which do not take account of administrative realities would prescribe. Many decisions with broader implications will be made far down in the organization. At the same time that is occurring, the manager will spend some of his time on routine work and some of it on matters seemingly remote from either the most pressing or most important concerns of the day. But they are all his responsibility.

ADMINISTRATIVE POINT OF VIEW

An understanding of the environment in which general managers work is essential in developing the attitudes and viewpoint that will make you effective in that job. That viewpoint, which distinguishes the observer from the participant and the specialist from the generalist, has often been called "The Administrative Point of View."

Many attempts have been made to define in more specific terms just what constitutes the administrative point of view. One would hope to be able to go beyond the judge who, in dealing with an obscenity case, declared "I may not able to define it, but I sure know it when I see it." Professor C. R. Christensen[5] has suggested the following elements as being critical to the administrative point of view:

1. A focus on understanding the specific situation.
2. A focus on the total situation, as well as the specific.
3. Sensitivity to interrelationships: the connectedness of all organizational functions and processes.
4. Examining and understanding any administrative situation from a multidimensional point of view.
5. Approaching problems as one responsible for the achievements of the organization.
6. An action orientation.

In order to be an effective manager or subordinate it is essential to have both the desire to understand the nature of the pressures the administrator has to deal with and the ability to put yourself in that position in order to deal with those pressures. It involves understanding the values, talents, and freedom of action of the administrator and those around him.

To be effective at analyzing problems and advising managers does not require placing managers on a pedestal in deference to their knowledge, skills, or intellectual abilities. Neither is it useful, however, to assume that you are so much smarter, better trained, or better informed than the managers you observe or read about that you can readily solve in a single class (perhaps three times a day) problems they have been dealing with for years. Effective analysis and action in the real organization is much more likely to stem from at least the beginning assumption that the managers involved understand their problems better than you do and act the way they do for reasons that are sound to them.

Intellectual and Administrative Skills

The process of policy formulation and administration requires a melding of intellectual and administrative skills. For example, identifying problems that affect the long-term position of the firm calls for the ability to select and relate a variety of information from a number of sources so that an inclusive statement of key problems can be made. Making such an analysis requires, however, more than the intellectual skill of analyzing environmental trends and quantitative data on internal corporate operations. It also requires the ability to incorporate "soft" data and judgments, some of it involving people and their abilities and motivation. Actionable alternatives must be developed that are understandable as well as acceptable and hopefully appealing to others. This ability depends upon what we can call an administrative sense. Most managerial decisions require a sense of what is administratively possible, not just what would be most desirable. The perfect plan that has no chance of being adopted in reality is not a very useful solution for the administrator.

The general manager does not have any all-wise advisor to identify what problem or problems he should be watching or working on at a particular time; that must be decided on personally. And there is no reference book to look into, no infallible aid to give *the* solution to most of the problems and tasks you do undertake. The most significant problems you will deal with are the ones that cannot readily be resolved by clear-cut analytical techniques or by others using their own knowledge and judgment. That is why they end up with you. As Professor Kenneth Andrews has commented,

> Many teachers and students find quantitative techniques and theoretical models easier to teach—intellectually fascinating, beguilingly self-contained, rigorous, and capable of being memorized and quickly applied, widely if not wisely. They forget to insist that for the most part only trivial management problems are neatly structured and quantifiable. All modeling and quantitative analyses directed at a decision are only preludes to subjective judgment. Vision must then transcend technique.[6]

"As Is" versus "Should Be"

It is your job to find some workable solution to the problems you are dealing with. In doing this you will have to deal with the "as is" of reality, not the "should be" of much theory. When theory and reality conflict with each other, you will have to be cautious indeed before you take refuge in the comfort and orderliness of theory in preference to the messiness of reality. Such decisions involve the exercise of judgment and will be improved by discussion and consultation with others. Unfortunately you will seldom be sure before your decision is made, and sometimes not even after it is made, that you have made the "right" or "best" decision.

The administrator must be willing and able to work in a climate of uncertainty, which is often uncomfortable. You will have to become accustomed to accepting the responsibility for important decisions reached under time pressure, on the basis of limited facts, and in the face of many unknowns. You will have to work with people who, like yourself, have some personal idiosyncrasies and professional limitations. Almost always, some associates or other parties involved will have different opinions about matters, and their views need to be taken into account. The administrator is usually in the lonesome situation of being the possessor of ultimate responsibility but with few people with whom he can share all of his thoughts and concerns. You will inevitably make some mistakes, as will your subordinates. The experienced administrator will hope to reach wise decisions most of the time but will expect and allow for the inevitable errors. The administrator who understands such an environment and is effective in working within it is a successful manager.

The administrative point of view consists of dealing with the manager and his problems, not the researcher or observer and his problems. It is a viewpoint essential to effective analysis and action in any organization. It is best learned on the job. It can most readily be taught by means of the case method, to which we will turn next.

CASE METHOD

The case method is widely used in executive development programs and is also commonly used in college and university courses that attempt to deal with problems in practice that have a significant administrative content. Indeed, it is difficult to learn to deal with the administrative context so important in practice in the absence of teaching material and classroom discussion that makes attention to that aspect of management possible and productive. The development of the administrative point of view is greatly facilitated by the requirement to apply your analyses and the knowledge you have gained elsewhere to a specific administrative situation.

What Cases Are

Cases, as used in the Business Policy courses at the Harvard Business School, generally are descriptions of an actual situation as of the time the case was written. Most are based on field research in the organization described; cases dealing primarily with the economic factors affecting strategy formulation are sometimes based only on published information. Cases are not traditional research documents which develop and test hypotheses; neither are they necessarily examples of the "right" or "wrong" answers to the problems described. Indeed, in some of the cases, as in much of practice, part of the problem is to identify and attach priorities to the problems.

Cases done with the cooperation of an organization are always released for use by that organization. Cases are sometimes disguised to preserve confidentiality, and the disguise may range from the altering of some quantitative data that the company does not want released (which is almost always noted in a footnote) to a disguise of company and individual names, places, and sometimes industries and products. The disguise may be so complete that an identification of either the actual industry or company is impossible. In all instances every attempt is made to preserve the significant issues and relationships that were important in the original situation.

Purpose of Cases

Cases are not meant to "stand alone," and very seldom is it possible to learn much from reading a single case without discussing it with someone. Cases are designed to be the raw material from which you can work out for yourself, under the guidance of a trained instructor and through discussion with your classmates, how you would approach that particular problem and what action you would take or recommendations you would make. The case is not designed to present you with a right answer which you can memorize in the hopes that you will remember it if you ever encounter a similar situation. Neither will you benefit greatly from listening to what others think is the right answer or the best approach; the development of understanding and skill is best accomplished by actively participating yourself in the search for solutions. Cases are the raw materials that permit simulation in the classroom of the actual discussions carried on informally among managers and in board and committee rooms.

We believe a course based upon a series of case discussions conducted with these objectives in mind is the most effective way in which to help you develop an analytical approach useful in the solution of the problems of general management and to improve your own skills in applying that approach. Essential to the development of such knowledge and skills is a trained instructor and some text material that will provide the guidance needed to lend order to the progression of situations and ideas in the materials selected. There are many books of cases and text in business policy or general management available, and a large number of different individual cases can be obtained from HBS Case Services and other sources.[7]

Preparing a Case for Class

The question of how one should prepare a case for class is a common one. As with other forms of preparation, there is no one "right" way that applies to everyone. Each of us must develop the methods that serve us best. Moreover, we all must change our approach somewhat to deal with each new case situation. There are, however, a few overall suggestions that may be useful.

You should first read the case through to get a general impression of what it is about, how it seems to come out, and what kinds of information it contains. You should also try to place the case in the context of the course and what kinds of issues you have been discussing, as the choice of the sequence of cases used in a course or program is seldom a casual matter. Cases have multiple uses, but the experienced instructor always tries to choose a sequence of cases that will make it possible for the learning in each case to cumulate as other cases are discussed.

There is a real advantage in doing this first reading a day or two before the time when you must do your thorough and final preparation. There is a value in having the general situation in mind in time to mull it over, both consciously and subconsciously, for a while. That is true of any important problem one has to deal with—in school, in business, anywhere.

For the second reading, we suggest you take the time to proceed slowly and carefully, studying the tables and exhibits, and making notes as you go. If the data are available, an analysis of the financial performance and position is important; suggestions on how to go about this are given in Chapter 5. Perhaps some headings will occur to you under which you want to summarize what you believe are especially pertinent factors.

When you feel you are about at the end of your preparation, it will be well to ask yourself if you could, if you had the chance to talk to the persons responsible for this company,

1. Talk intelligently with them about their company and their job in managing it.
2. Show them why the main issues you have distilled as a result of your analysis are really of first importance.
3. Give them a coordinated program of action that would be practical and would have a reasonable chance to succeed.

We urge you to discuss the cases with one another, if possible, while preparing them. Managers in business discuss their problems with other key people. One of the things you will learn from a discussion of cases is that you will almost always be able to improve your own analysis and solution as a result of listening to, and especially participating in, a discussion of the problem with others. Be sure you do your own independent work and independent thinking, however, as that is how the most effective learning is achieved. Do not be too stubborn to recognize a better idea than your own, but be sure you really understand and believe in it before you adopt it.

A Little More Information

Cases dealing with the problems of the general manager are often long. There is almost always a need to have some information about the industry and its competitive conditions, the company and its background, as well as its present position, the particular problem(s) that may be of concern, and the people in the company and the context in which they work. In spite of the length, however, you may frequently feel that more information of a particular type would be very useful to you in reaching a decision.

That might be true, but you should form the habit of working with the information available and making sure that you make the best use of what you have, which in the well-written case will be ample for your purposes. You are not likely to have all of the information you would like when you have to make a decision based on a case situation, but you are unlikely to have that as a manager either. More information is always available but usually at a cost in terms of both time and money. The ability to judge when you have enough information to enable you to make a reasoned decision is an important skill for a manager to acquire.

If you feel more information is essential, make some reasonable assumptions and state them explicitly. It should never be necessary to go to the library for additional information; a case is not meant to be either a complete history as of the date of the case or a bulletin incorporating all of the latest happenings. Information about what a company actually did or how decisions actually turned out is likely to be far less useful in developing the general analytical approach you are seeking than is the struggle of working with the facts presented to you to solve the problems as of the time of the case.

Your Role

It is important for you to attempt to understand and adopt the position of the involved general manager in each of the cases. At times you will be asked to assume that YOU are the "person on the spot"; at times you will be asked to ADVISE the manager—either as a subordinate or as a consultant. In any event, it is essential for you to establish the habit of asking yourself what actions you would take or advise in *this specific situation*, and then deal with the uncertainties, conflicts, constraints, unknowns, and ambiguities as best you can—just as the practicing general manager must do.

READINGS

A number of readings that you may find useful in the study of general management are listed in Appendix A. We have not included reading suggestions at the end of each chapter, as few readings address directly the concerns of single chapters.

If you are studying cases in a course or a seminar, your primary emphasis should be on the identification and solution of the specific problems as you find them in the cases. You will probably have been exposed to a number of courses and many readings dealing with various aspects of business administration prior to this. The principal task before you now is to draw upon the materials and techniques with which you are already familiar, as well as background readings your instructor may suggest, to assist you in the solution of the problems found in specific cases. Your objective should be to develop an understanding of an approach to the analysis and solution of the problems of the general manager via the study of a series of specific cases, not to learn what various authors have to say about general classes of problems.

SUMMARY

The type of learning this book is designed to help you with consists of developing proficiency in analyzing general management problems, developing skills in advising managers, and ultimately acting in that role yourself. An understanding of the nature of the job and the development of what we have termed "The Administrative Point of View" is a prerequisite to the development of those skills. Listening to or reading about the solutions developed by others will do little to develop those skills. We will turn in the next chapter to the concept of strategy, a central element in the development of an analytical approach to the job of the general manager.

PART 2

The Single-Business Company

CHAPTER 2

Strategy: The Concept

In this chapter we will help you develop an understanding of the term *strategy* that will be useful to you in increasing your knowledge of the job of the general manager and in beginning to develop the skills, both analytical and administrative, that are important in the performance of that job. Our focus as we develop the concept in this chapter and present an approach to the formulation of strategy in the next several chapters will primarily be with the single-business firm and the functional form of organization. The application of the concept and the approach to diversified firms will be discussed in Part 3 of the book.

Since so much of your time as a general manager will be spent developing and implementing the strategy of the firm, it is surely worth some effort to try to define the concept in operational terms. A statement of strategy should convey what a company is trying to achieve as well the broad outline of how it hopes to achieve it. The supporting plan for achieving the objectives specified in the strategy should specify what major steps are to be taken, in what rough time frame, by whom, what resources will be required, and how the resources will be obtained. The statement of strategy should communicate, in as tangible a way as possible, just how this particular company has chosen to compete in the marketplace.

More important than a memorized definition, however, is the development of an understanding of the concept that will enable you to make use of it in your role as general manager to enhance the performance of the firm. The best way to develop an understanding of what a statement of strategy should include in the specific case is to begin with the purposes an explicit statement of strategy can serve for the organization. Such a statement will be of great help in:

1. Forcing disciplined attention to the development of explicit long-term objectives for the firm.
2. Developing the sequence of steps over time by which these long-term objectives can be achieved.
3. Providing guidance for the organizational efforts required to implement the selected strategy.

QUANTIFICATION AND CLASSIFICATION

Although many aspects of a statement of strategy can and should be expressed in quantitative terms, as, for example, earnings or growth goals, it unfortunately is no more possible to assign a number to a strategy than it is to the health of an individual. That a definition precise enough to enable you to specify an overall strategy in quantitative terms—a key step in many of the advances in the physical sciences—neither exists nor seems likely to occur should neither discourage nor detain you.

Neither is it possible to develop classification schemes for strategies that are as rigorous or useful as those that have been developed for the plant and animal kingdoms. Although many ways of classifying and comparing strategies are possible, few provide useful guidance when the purpose shifts from the logic of the classification scheme to the usefulness of prescriptions based on it.

There are three broad categories of strategies that you may find useful, however. As explained more fully by Porter,[1] three potentially successful generic strategies that may contribute to competitive success are those based on overall cost leadership, a differentiation of the product, or a focus on specific buyer groups. Although no classification scheme can displace the need for judgment and analysis applied to the specific situation, it may provide a useful starting point.

A number of Japanese products, for example, have gained a large market share in the United States within the past decade in large part because of a significant cost advantage. In the case of automobiles, Japanese manufacturers are estimated to have a landed cost advantage over American manufacturers on the order of $1,500 to $2,000 per car. When combined with considerable perceived product differentiation with regard to quality and performance, the reasons for the Japanese success in the United States markets and the depressed conditions in the American automobile industry become clearer. So does the difficulty of devising an appropriate competitive response on the part of the American manufacturers, if the cost differential cannot be eliminated because of significantly higher capital and labor costs.

Not all competitors in a given industry need follow the same generic strategy in order to be successful. To remain with the auto industry, both Mercedes-Benz and BMW have done exceedingly well in terms of sales and profits, but neither is a low-cost manufacturer, nor do they compete primarily on price. For them, the combination of a highly differentiated product and the loyalty of a specific market segment have overcome the liability of a consumer price double or more what one would need to pay for functionally similar American automobiles.

Another common way of classifying strategies is with regard to the growth goals relative to the growth of the market. Such strategies are often categorized as "gain share," "hold share," or "yield share." Much attention has been given to the conditions under which various growth strategies are most appropriate, especially for the diversified company with a number of products in its portfolio with different growth opportunities. These issues will be discussed further in Chapter 14.

In order for any strategy to generate above-average economic performance over the long run, however, there is strong reason to believe that it must be based on a comparative advantage based on some combination of low cost, product differentiation, or market segmentation. It does not follow, unfortunately, that building on the above relative advantages guarantees success. The nature of competition within the industry and the growth potentials that exist will have a major impact on profitability and growth.

For example, the presence of two or more strong, low-cost competitors, both fighting for market share in a rapidly growing industry, can ensure profit problems for all until strategies are changed or a winner emerges. A recent example occurred in the summer of 1983, when Texas Instruments unexpectedly announced a $100 million loss for their second quarter earnings, attributed largely to losses from their aggressive entry into the already overcrowded home computer business. The stock fell from $158 to $107 per share within only two days—a decline of 32 percent and an overall decline in the market value of the company of over a billion dollars. Prices of home computers had declined by 75 percent in 18 months, and the explosive growth of the market had not yet resulted in comparable growth in profits for most of the many competitors in the industry.

Some classification of strategies into the manner in which competitive advantage will be sought and the growth goals that are appropriate is useful. Rather than develop more detailed classification schemes for strategies, however, we will turn next to a consideration of the elements that should commonly be included in a statement of strategy that will be useful for business purposes.

SELECTION OF OBJECTIVES

One major component of the statement of strategy is the specification of the long-term, basic objectives of the total enterprise or major business unit. Many writers use the terms *goals* and *objectives* interchangeably; others carefully ascribe different meanings to them. The distinction is not important as long as the way in which the terms are used is clear. The basic, long-term goals or objectives for a company should include such items as desirable levels of growth, profits, and risk; broad definitions of the industries or products the company intends to engage in; and, if possible, something which captures the somewhat intangible character of the enterprise. The important point to remember is that the general manager has both the responsibility for and some ability to influence the longer-term, basic objectives of the firm. These are seldom fixed by law, practice, or edict. That objectives with regard to growth and profitability goals as well as lines of business and manner of competing vary widely among companies is a matter of common observation. We think it will be more fruitful for you to attempt to discover in the specific companies you are interested in what these objectives seem to be, and what they might be, rather than attempt to define exactly what the term *objectives* should include in all cases.

This definition of strategy, though common to business, is unlike that used by most military writers. The military definition most often accepts an objective or a goal as fixed and often imposed by a higher authority and views a strategy as a means of achieving that objective. Unlike general managers, who not only get to choose their wars but also, within limits, define what constitutes success, generals are charged with winning the wars assigned to them. The greater freedom that the general manager has in choosing his objectives adds a level of complexity to the task, however, just as the assignment to write a paper on "a topic of your choice" is not always viewed as being granted a favor. Since the general manager must be concerned not only with how to achieve objectives but also with what the objectives should be, the development of these objectives is part of the task of developing a statement of strategy for the firm.

The determination of these longer-term objectives is both important and difficult. Objectives that turn out to be too high in terms of growth or profits can have severely damaging effects on an otherwise healthy business because of the pressures they create to change the basic nature of the business or to take excessive risks. On the other hand, objectives which are too low in view of the opportunities open to the firm and its own resources will be less challenging to the members of the firm and will likely result in reduced economic performance. More important for the longer run, it may also cause an unnecessary loss of market position and competitive strength.

Objectives stated at the level of abstraction of "grow as fast as possible," or "maximize the earnings per share," or "maximize the long-run value of the common shareholder's interest," useful though they may be to the economist or social scientist in need of tractable models of the firm or of the economy, are seldom a solution to the above difficulties. Without considerable elaboration, they do little more than point a direction for those who must translate an objective into operational terms. They communicate little about the acceptable level of risk or the character of the business, for example, and provide even less help in the task of translating a strategy into terms which will have meaning to the managers and employees of the business as they go about their work.

ACHIEVEMENT OF OBJECTIVES

A second major purpose of a strategy is to develop and make explicit the means by which the firm can achieve the objectives it has selected. An examination of those objectives will lead to an identification of the factors that are likely to play a role in their achievement and, therefore, those factors that should receive explicit attention. The result should be the development of a plan, or sequence of steps over time, with appropriate checkpoints and contingency plans, that will hopefully enable the firm to accomplish its long-term objectives.

Products and Services

In order to make possible the development of a plan of action, a statement of strategy should include something about the nature of the products, not only in the literal terms of what the product is called and is made of, but of what service it provides to the consumer. What, if anything, is distinctive about the product or service? Is it high or low quality, relatively high or low volume, designed for a broad market or a selected portion of the market, and is it rapidly changing or relatively stable? Are we emphasizing function or fashion? Do we offer a limited line or a full line? How important is advertising and promotion to the product or service provided? How, if at all, can our product be distinguished from present and potential competing products or services? The particular dimensions selected for describing the product will vary with the product. It is important, however, that you find a way to move beyond the label of "autos" or "watches" or "writing instruments" to a more detailed description of the product, the function it is to serve, and the market segment it is intended to appeal to.

Financing

The means of financing the enterprise is important, not only with respect to the present, but even more so with regard to the way in which future requirements will be met. Growth requires increased assets, which can only come from internal sources (primarily, retained earnings) or external sources. In qualitative terms, what degree of risk is acceptable? More specifically, what maximum proportion of debt can we get and will we tolerate in the capital structure, what level of dividends do we want to pay and with what certainty, and how willing are we to risk having to sell stock at depressed prices, sell a portion of the assets, or even be forced to merge with another company if things do not work out as planned? Growth objectives which result in financial requirements in excess of what the firm can earn in the marketplace or of what investors and lenders will willingly advance it raise substantially the risks for management of losing control and for shareholders of losing money.

Integration and Scale

In addition to the nature of the product or service and the means by which we will finance the business, it is important to know specifically how the product or service will be provided. Are we a manufacturer or primarily an assembler of purchased parts? To what extent have we integrated backward to provide for our own sources of supply or raw materials—as in the case of steel producers owning coal and iron ore mines—and to what extent have we integrated forward to control our channels of distribution, as in the case of a farm equipment dealer—Massey-Ferguson, for example—owning some of its dealerships? To what extent do we seek and need to take advantage of economies of scale in manufacturing via standard products, high volume, long production runs, and few locations, as contrasted with seeking to command a higher price in the market as a result of being a more specialized, lower-volume, but higher cost manufacturer?

Functional Policies

Included in a statement of corporate strategy should be some attention to the commitment of resources to and the policies to be followed in the major functional departments of the company.

Polaroid, for example, during its many years of rapid growth as the only company offering instant photographic products to the consumer, invested as little as possible in manufacturing assets, preferring instead to subcontract as much as possible of both film and camera manufacturing. Capital investments were made only in the critical or truly proprietary aspects of manufacturing, and even these facilities were often leased. The financial resources and management time thus made available were applied to their research and product development activities, as they believed these to be far more important to their long-run success than competence in manufacturing. Marketing policies largely ignored dealers and distributors and concentrated instead on the ultimate consumer. In contrast to others in the industry, Polaroid never licensed any of its developments to others and sought instead to defend its exclusive position in instant photography by means of an extensive wall of patent protection around its products. The company avoided all long-term debt and never gave any indication (under the leadership of Dr. Land) of any significant interest in any form of diversification.[2]

Alfred Sloan, by way of contrast, described the strategy of General Motors in the 1920s as being one of balanced attention to all of the functional areas of their business. He believed—quite correctly, as it turned out—that long-run success in the automotive business at that time was more likely to result from such a balance rather than by attempting to excel in any one functional area. The strategy of balance among the functional areas was based on a conviction that any temporary successes that might result from a concentration on innovative engineering, styling, or marketing, as many competitors were doing, ran the risk of insufficient attention to other areas and therefore poorer performance in the long run.[3]

Lincoln Electric Company, a highly successful manufacturer of electric arc welding machines and supplies, defines its strategy very simply as seeking to provide a high-quality, well-defined product and service at a price lower than competition by means of a low overall cost position, made possible by a high and growing market share earned as a result of passing cost savings on to customers each year. Product development, manufacturing, and marketing, with a strong emphasis on customer service, are all considered of equal importance. Their unusual organizational policies, described further in Chapter 8, contribute significantly to the achievement of their strategy.[4]

The point is not that there is any such thing as a "right" or "ideal" statement of strategy and supporting functional policies, but that great variation is possible. It may be advantageous in view of the opportunities in the marketplace and the strategies of your competitors to devote resources to develop an advantage or a distinctive

competence in the research and development department, the manufacturing operations, the financial controls, the marketing department, or the personnel policies. Developing such a distinctive
competence or competitive advantage takes time and money and
management attention, however, and there is no simple formula that
will enable you to find the right combination.

Relatively few companies have the luxury of having, or realisti-
cally aspiring to, the dominant positions in overall size, cost position, or market share suggested by most analytical schemes as being
necessary to success. For most companies, the formulation of a strategy requires considerable attention and thought to the issue of how
to compete against larger competitors with greater resources and
greater potential for economies of scale in research and development, manufacturing, marketing, or management. The challenge you
will face as a general manager is to establish policies for the major
functional areas so that they are consistent with each other and
contribute to the achievement of the overall objectives of your specific company.

Organizing Concept

The final contribution that a statement of strategy will provide for
you in your role as a general manager is to help you develop an
organizing concept and central theme with regard to mobilizing the
organization in the accomplishment of the strategic objectives. Just
as the functional policies should be designed to be consistent with
each other and to support the strategy, the policies with regard to the
organization structure and processes should also be consistent with
each other and supportive of the strategy chosen. We will turn to
this task of implementation of strategy in Chapters 8 and 9.

SUMMARY

A well-developed and explicit strategy is well worth the considerable time and trouble it takes to develop it. The choice of the products and markets in which to compete, and the basis for competing
in them, are of crucial importance to a company. These propositions
are difficult to prove because of the myriad of internal and external
variables that affect company performance, including the catchall
"luck." It is certainly far more difficult to find either evidence or
logic that would support the opposite position, however, that the
choice of markets and ways to compete in them is of little consequence to a company.

The time and effort executives devote to matters of strategy and
the money companies spend for strategic consulting services should

be ample evidence of the importance practicing managers attach to the development of their corporate strategy. An experienced and highly successful group vice president of a major diversified industrial company stated his conclusion that the most important thing for him to do when he takes over the responsibilities for a new division, often in a business in which he has had no previous experience, is to develop, along with the division management, an explicit, brief statement of what the current strategy of the division is before making any attempts to evaluate or change that strategy. We would encourage you to attempt the same as you encounter new situations.

Responsibility for and participation in the strategy formulation process is a key responsibility of the general manager. That participation is essential not only because the outcome is important to the company, but also because the general manager brings both a perspective and a level of authority to the task that is likely to result in a better strategy as well as better acceptance of the strategy within the organization. Responsibility for and participation in does not mean, of course, that the general manager has to do all of the work; for anything but the smallest or simplest business, that would result in a superficial analysis. What it does mean is that the general manager of any company, no matter how large, clearly must understand the key problems and opportunities facing the company, enlist the help of line managers and staff and perhaps outsiders in collecting and analyzing the information needed and in developing possible courses of action, and then visibly support the choices made. Staff and subordinate assistance is helpful and often essential; but without the involvement and commitment of the general manager to the results, the staff work is likely to be ineffective. The single greatest hazard facing both the professional corporate planner and the company whose chief executive turns too much of the task of developing the corporate strategy over to the long-range planning department is that the resulting 200-page five-year plan, which may by all objective standards be an excellent plan, will gather dust rather than precipitate action.

We have thus far focused primarily on the purpose and content of a statement of corporate strategy and have said very little about how one might move from simply identifying the strategy of a company to evaluating it and making recommendations for changes. Developing and explaining an approach to this which you can apply to both case situations and actual practice is the principal purpose of the next several chapters.

CHAPTER 3

An Approach to
Strategy Formulation

In this chapter we will present a simple conceptual scheme that will be of help to you in identifying, evaluating, and making recommendations for changes in the strategy of the firm. It has been our experience that practicing general managers, their subordinates, and consultants to management all can make their efforts to influence corporate strategy more effective by the conscious use of a conceptual scheme or framework of analysis to assist them in the task.

COMPLEXITY

The strategy of the firm at any particular time is the product of a wide range of factors, including history, happenstance, oversight, external forces, and the conscious efforts of management to develop and influence that strategy. The problems of formulating strategy for a firm can be complex in the extreme. The many variables which should be taken into account include technical, economic, political, and social factors that may affect the business, now or in the future. The difficulty of obtaining reliable estimates for many of these variables is great. Predicting how the variables will interact with and influence each other as well as affect the overall performance of the firm requires not only facts and analysis but judgment.

As has become increasingly evident during the decade of the 70s, your analysis must also span continents. Strategic factors affecting industries and competitors affecting American companies have increasingly become international in origin. As is evident from the alarming declines in output, market share, and profitability in large and traditionally strong American industries—such as consumer electronics, autos, and steel—in the late 70s and early 80s, competition in many products is becoming increasingly global in nature, a trend persuasively presented in an article by Levitt.[1]

Formulating strategy in an analytical fashion will require that you take many diverse factors into account and also that you make judgments about these factors for many years in the future as well as in the present. You will have to deal with the uncertainty of tomorrow as well as with the complexity of today.

Some may be willing to venture firm opinions on short notice and with little apparent deliberation about the strategy firms in the auto industry should have adopted in the early or mid-70s to avoid the debacle of the late 70s and early 80s. During that period Chrysler survived only with government assistance; Ford and General Motors lost record amounts of money; and reduced production, layoffs, and terminations became major political and economic issues for the country. Others may not be hesitant at all to specify just how electric utility companies should take into account changing environmental regulations, high capital costs, rising and unpredictable fuel costs, strong public reaction against nuclear power, and increasing consumer opposition to rate increases and still generate enough capital to build plants needed in the next decades. In attempting to develop answers to such problems, however, all but the few true geniuses among us will find some sort of general framework or approach useful, if not essential.

We would like to suggest an approach to analysis which is simple to state and of wide applicability, but which nevertheless requires thoughtfulness, practice, and hard work to apply effectively. The approach presented here has been developed over several decades principally as a result of the research, teaching, and consulting activities of the faculty of the Business Policy course at the Harvard Business School, enriched by the ideas, experiences, and writings of others challenged by similar problems. Professor Kenneth Andrews has been the most articulate of those involved in the development of this still-evolving framework of analysis, which is now widely used.[2]

The approach we suggest is designed to help you simplify a complex task so that you can deal with it more effectively. We are trying to simplify the complex, not provide complex models for simplified problems. It is not a model that would meet the standards of many of our academic colleagues in the natural sciences or those with strong interests in quantitative methods, as neither the individual elements of the model nor the relationships among them can be quantified to any great extent. To our knowledge no such comprehensive model useful to general managers exists. What we do propose is an approach which will encourage and make possible disciplined attention to several major areas of importance by the busy general manager faced with the real-life task of formulating and evaluating the corporate strategy of the firm.

APPROACH

The approach we have found both general enough to be applicable in a wide number of situations as well as specific enough to be useful in individual and unique situations states that the formulation of strategy of a company should be based on a consideration of four main items: relevant facts and trends in the environment, the resources available to the company, the values of the management group, and the responsibilities felt toward society for the achievement of noneconomic goals. These factors, which have to be evaluated in relation to each other in the formulation of strategy, can be portrayed as shown in the left-hand side of Exhibit 3–1:

EXHIBIT 3–1
Formulation and Implementation of Strategy

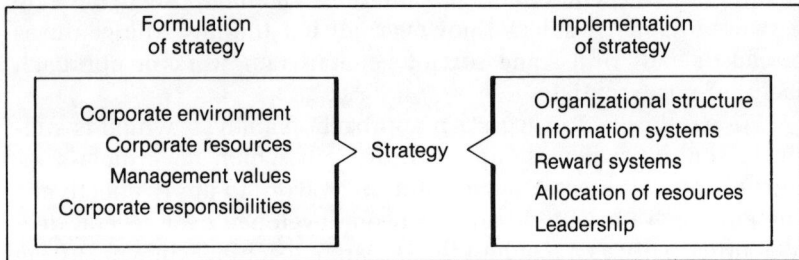

Formulation of strategy		Implementation of strategy
Corporate environment Corporate resources Management values Corporate responsibilities	> Strategy <	Organizational structure Information systems Reward systems Allocation of resources Leadership

The right-hand side of this exhibit deals with the implementation of strategy, a process we have repeatedly emphasized as closely related to strategy formulation in practice. The range of strategies that could reasonably be pursued is most certainly limited by what the organization, even under the best of conditions, could be expected to accomplish. In addition, no strategy, even after being adopted, can be effective until the organization becomes committed to the objectives sought and the means by which they can be achieved. We will describe the approach to implementation further in Chapters 8 and 9.

Exhibit 3–1 reduces to the simplest level possible the broad areas of concern to the general manager in the formulation and implementation of corporate strategy. Much more complicated conceptual schemes are possible, and the above can easily be made more detailed. It is our experience, however, that the creative and thoughtful application of the simple model shown above is generally preferable to the use of more elaborate models, with the attendant risk of losing sight of what is important in the specific situation.

The process of formulating a strategy should consist of an assessment of the relevant facts and trends occurring within each of these major areas, a judgment of the ways in which these areas will or can be made to influence each other, and the creative development of a strategy, including the selection of longer-term objectives, suited to the unique situation of the particular company. The strategy which results from this process should allow for the trends in the company's environment, including the actions of competitors; take advantage of the strengths and minimize the effects of the company's weaknesses; allow for the personal values and aspirations of those managers who are in a position to influence the company; and make provision for what the company either wants to do or should do in view of what may be expected of it by the broader society of which it is a part. Each of these factors will be discussed in more detail in later chapters.

As you proceed to identify, evaluate, and recommend changes in the strategy of the company you are studying or working in, you should keep in mind the three deceptively simple questions you should always try to answer with regard to each unique situation that you study:

1. Where are we now?
2. Where do we want to go?
3. How do we get there?

The approach described above will help you arrive at reasoned answers to the above questions, but not in a mechanical or deterministic way; it provides neither checklists nor yes–no questions. It is our experience that such seeming expedients make it less rather than more likely that the creative job that needs to be done will take place.

Neither does the approach ensure that you will arrive at a demonstrably right answer, but that is a reflection of the difficulties of formulating strategy in real life as opposed to strategies for competing in a computer simulation model or a chess game. No approach of which we are aware does guarantee the right answer; experienced and intelligent executives will often disagree in difficult strategic situations. If systematically and carefully followed, however, the approach will result in the logic and assumptions underlying strategic recommendations becoming more explicit and clear to all. This, in turn, has several significant benefits.

First of all, it permits a more detailed and reasoned examination or dissection of the basis for differing strategic recommendations for the same situation. The quality of the assumptions and the logic, as well as the choices being made with regard to levels of risk, profits, growth, and so on, can more readily be isolated and discussed. To say that an approach does not guarantee a single, "right" answer is not to say that some strategic recommendations will not, upon examination, be judged by most to be of higher quality than others.

Second, because the entire process of strategy formulation is made more explicit, improving one's skills at that process becomes easier. Intuitive approaches by experienced and skillful managers may result in brilliant strategies, but such intuitive abilities are not easy to acquire, either by birth or practice. Some of the most difficult and important decisions you will make as a manager will involve a substantial combination of intuition, creativity, inspiration, artistry, and judgment. Students as well as executives, however, benefit from expanding rather than reducing the explicit and analytical portion of the strategy formulation process and improving their skills at that portion through practice. Because strategic decisions by their very nature are not made frequently, are seldom made by aspiring executives early in their careers, and often require the passage of many years or even decades before their wisdom and quality can be evaluated, practice and skill in making strategic decisions are not easy to come by. Breaking down the process of making those decisions and participating, when possible, in that process will facilitate the development of the skills and experience that will be valuable to you as you help others on that key aspect of the job of the general manager, or perform the task yourself.

Finally, an evaluation of both the strategy itself as well as the progress of the organization in carrying out that strategy are facilitated. Conditions change, unforeseen obstacles as well as opportunities arise, and achievement inevitably exceeds hopes and plans in some respects and falls short in others. Periodic reevaluation of progress as well as of the strategy itself is essential, both to provide guidance to the manager in leading the organization in the implementation of strategy and in making whatever changes seem necessary in the strategy itself.

INTERRELATIONSHIP OF FORMULATION AND IMPLEMENTATION

In focusing on the steps to go through in formulating a corporate strategy, we are temporarily ignoring other aspects of the general manager's job. Once again, let us caution that strategic problems in practice seldom appear, nor are they addressed, in isolation of the problems associated with implementing that strategy within the organization. The two activities are intertwined in real life, and the effective manager must constantly move back and forth between the tasks of the implementation of the existing strategy and the continual examination and reassessment of that strategy.

The analytical approach to the general manager's job we are developing is not intended to be a description of the manager's daily activities; the two are vastly different. A typical day in the life of a general manager is surprisingly fragmented, frantic, and disorderly, as is well documented by Kotter.[3] The need for an approach that can bring some order to such unavoidable chaos should be apparent. The fact that educational courses and the teaching cases within the courses can be organized to deal with only one part of the manager's job at a time should not mislead you into believing that an effective way to study and learn about a task in the classroom is also a description of the task in practice.

In the development and presentation of an analytical approach to the broad and complex job of the general manager, we have chosen to concentrate first on a portion of that job, the formulation of strategy, for two reasons. First, developing your skills and understanding of this task can best take place by means of some concentration on that portion of the general manager's job. We all learn best by splitting up a large task and learning portions of it at a time. Second, even the most experienced general manager can best make progress in the performance of his tasks by concentrating first on one and then on another aspect of the job. Even though problems are interrelated, few of us can work effectively on everything at once. Effective management, however, requires attention to the totality, not just a concentration on a part of the whole.

SEQUENCE OF STEPS

Although the approach we are suggesting breaks down the task of formulating strategy into an examination of four broad areas, we do not want to give the impression that it is a sequential, "one-time through" procedure in which you can in turn analyze the environment, assess the strengths and weaknesses of the company, ascertain the values and aspiration of the management, allow for social expectations, and produce strategic recommendations which will be good for some substantial period of time. Such a procedure does not correspond with practice, or at least with good practice, in two respects: each major factor must be investigated in relation to the others, and the process is a never-ending one.

The basic nature of the strategy will hopefully remain constant over substantial periods of time; but changing industry conditions, company performance, and competitive moves make continual examination and readjustment of the competitive posture essential. The major strategic evaluations and adjustments take place during the annual planning cycle in most companies. In the better companies and the more dynamic industries, however, there is constant attention to the need to make adjustments between the annual planning periods. When businesses are in a period of rapid change—for example, electronic calculators in the mid-70s and personal computers in the early 80s—one can read almost every week of the technological and pricing moves and responses of the major competitors.

SUMMARY

The formulation of strategy in an analytical manner involves the consideration of a wide range of factors: technical, economic, political, and social. The way in which these factors develop in the future is the important question, but that can only be judged from a consideration of the past and the present. Some factors will be relatively easy to predict or perhaps not critical, anyway; others may be both important and highly uncertain. In addition, the increasingly global nature of industrial competition makes it essential to look far beyond your own borders in assessing these factors and their importance to your company.

   Strategy formulation in practice is a continuous process, separable from but not independent of the ongoing administrative problems and characteristics of the company. It is a process of continual examination and adjustment of interrelated elements, not a series of discrete puzzles to be solved independently of each other and in sequence. Because it is a complex task involving many variables that in turn require much judgment to interpret intelligently and to relate to each other, an approach or conceptual scheme which directs your attention in a disciplined manner to an orderly examination of the data will be useful to you. We will turn in succeeding chapters to more detailed suggestions for assessing each of these major factors, beginning with the analysis of the environment in the next chapter.

CHAPTER 4

Strategy Formulation and Corporate Environment

$\mathbf{T}$he importance of looking at the overall environment of a company should not require any elaboration. The issue is not whether to look, but what to look at, how to predict what is likely to happen or can be made to happen, and what effect these happenings might have on a specific company. The *environment* is listed first in the approach to strategy formulation that we encourage you to use, but that is a matter of choice rather than necessity. It could be investigated after a thorough examination of the strengths and weaknesses of the company, for example, but we have found that in most cases it is better to proceed from a broad investigation of the industry in which a firm competes to a more detailed examination of the firm itself.

A comprehensive investigation of the industry should include careful attention to actual and potential competitors. The evaluation of competitors can be carried out using the same methods of analysis you apply to your own company. Judgments concerning your own strategy should always incorporate an evaluation of the position, probable motives, and options of your major competitors. For that reason, we will discuss competitors again in the next chapter, following the discussion on evaluating the strengths and weaknesses of a company.

WHAT IS "OUR INDUSTRY"?

By *environment* we generally mean all of those factors external to the company which do or could have an important influence on the performance of the company. Such factors can be classified into economic, technical, political, and social categories, but a rigid separation is not necessary. Of more importance is developing the ability to select what should be examined so that the task can be accomplished by ordinary mortals in the course of all of the other demands on their time and thoughts. In order to do this, workable industry boundaries need to be created.

It is true but of little help to observe that the world increasingly is becoming one large, interrelated system in which happenings anywhere may have an impact on any business. It is also true, however, that events and developments which may not be apparent in the everyday course of business may nevertheless have a significant impact on us. The announcement of the development of the semiconductor by Bell Laboratories in 1948 and the commercialization of the devices by firms relatively unknown in the electronics industry of the time resulted in much more than just the demise of vacuum tubes. Entire new products, industries, and major companies arose, as any comparison of a current list of companies in the electronics and computing businesses with a similar list of 25 years ago would indicate. These companies in turn have come to see some of their markets dominated, or at least strongly influenced, by foreign competitors that were hardly deemed a threat in the early years of growth of the new industry.

To use a simple example, Kueffel & Esser, the dominant producer of the precision slide rules bought by every college student in sciences, engineering, or business administration a generation ago, has seen its market taken over completely by electronic calculators. Calculators are based on a totally different technology and manufacturing process. In addition, they were developed and marketed by companies such as Texas Instruments and Hewlett-Packard, who were formerly not even remote competitors of K&E. Few users of calculators today would even recognize the K&E logo, let alone know how to use one of their slide rules.

When viewed over the perspective of decades, similar examples can be found in many other industries. Timex, a company which had manufactured many mechanical timing devices during World War II, developed and introduced on the American market an extremely low-priced but reliable, mass-produced mechanical watch in the 1950s. The Swiss watch industry, which had long dominated the free world markets with their high-quality, high-priced mechanical watches sold largely as jewelry items that would last a lifetime or two, was very slow to recognize and respond to the competitive threat. Alternately ignoring and scorning Timex and its original concept of a cheap, functional watch that users could throw away rather than repair after a few years, the Swiss saw their market share and profits erode seriously. As the Swiss belatedly tried to catch up to Timex, which upgraded the quality and price of their watches and moved into even more direct competition with the traditional Swiss watches, both were seriously affected by the development of the electronic watch by companies not formerly in the watch business.

The environment consists of a spectrum of facts and circumstances, some immediately observable and obviously important and some with such low probability of impact on us that we can safely ignore them in order to deal more effectively with what we can perceive and comprehend. It is essential to recognize that limits must be drawn and that the limits must be defined in terms of the specific company and its strategy and products, not just a general notion of the industry. You will have to strike a balance between the risks of lost opportunities and unseen threats that may come from defining the limits too narrowly and the intellectual paralysis that accompanies the attempt to include everything.

The principal reason for defining an industry in operational terms for each specific company situation you encounter is the need to identify present and potential competitive products and services, principal competitors, and the important factors affecting the demand for the products and services of that industry and the operations of the companies that meet this demand. BIC Pen rose to prominence and prosperity in the ballpoint pen field from an entry position of virtual bankruptcy in 1958 with the old "Waterman Pen" name as its principal asset. When should the old-line companies such as Scheaffer, Parker, and Scripto that had long dominated the writing instrument field have recognized the importance of new BIC strategy, and how could they have responded more effectively?

The classic battle between Polaroid and Kodak in the instant photography field provides an even more dramatic example of the emergence of a technology and a competitor from inconspicuous beginnings. When a young and small Polaroid offered in 1948 a brown-and-white (later black-and-white) instant print of lower quality and at a higher price than conventional prints by the huge and well-established Kodak, were the companies really competitors? At what point did instant photography compete significantly with conventional photography for the same consumer dollar, as is clearly the case by the time of the introduction of an instant camera by Kodak in 1976? When should both have become more concerned about the inroads of the Japanese in both instant and conventional photography rather than the moves and countermoves against each other?

That the problem of assessing both opportunity and threats involves the monitoring of foreign competition as well as technological developments is well demonstrated by the large inroads of Far

Eastern, and primarily Japanese, entrants into markets formerly dominated by American producers. How you define the industry has a major influence on the size and projected growth of the market, who you consider your potential as well as present competitors to be, what trends and developments are likely to be relevant, and the probable opportunities and threats facing the company.

ECONOMIC CHARACTERISTICS

After you have defined an industry sufficiently well to identify competitive products, services, and the companies that provide them, you will want to investigate the economic performance of the industry. What is the approximate size of the market, at what rate has it been growing, what is the average level of profitability of the industry, and how much do these vary from year to year?

The general level of profitability within an industry is obviously of interest, as it describes the returns that are likely to be available to the "average" competitor. These levels vary among industries, over time within an industry, and of course by firms within the industry in any given year. To get some sense of how great the variations are and how they change over time, you would find it most instructive to look at such measures in the yearly Fortune 500 listings.

One reason the size of the market is important is because the volume of business reasonably obtainable clearly has implications for the investment that can be undertaken to enter or compete in that market. A small market cannot justify high research, advertising, or capital expenditures no matter how successful the efforts are; conversely, a large market potential may justify, if the company wishes to try, large investments. Indeed, large markets often attract large investments and therefore large companies, a fact of which most small companies are well aware.

Another reason for concern with size is that many companies prefer not to bother with ventures which may be difficult to manage and which, even if successful, are unlikely to grow large enough to have a significant effect on the overall operations of the company. Small companies often justify seeking specialized market niches for this very reason—in the hope that larger companies will not find it worthwhile to do battle in such small markets.

One example of such a competitive structure would be the existence of hundreds of small, local can-making companies in an industry in which the larger production runs are exclusively the province of multibillion companies like American Can, Continental Can, and the Crown Cork and Seal Company. The small companies are not able to compete with the big on the large orders, but the big do not find it worthwhile to compete with the small for the size of order they can efficiently handle.

The relationship between market size and company sales to that market, or the share of market (SOM), is also important for reasons beyond simply economies of scale and issues of market power. It is an indication of the degree to which your growth will be limited by the growth potential of the overall market. The larger the share of the market that you have, the more difficult it becomes to grow faster than the overall market. A competitor with a small share of a market, on the other hand, is limited only by the extent to which it can take market share away from the larger competitors.

The growth potential of the market is important for a number of reasons. Foremost, of course, is that a growing market may provide sufficient opportunity for all of the competitors to achieve satisfactory rates of growth from the expanding market rather than from each other. Company growth secured from an expanding market rather than at the expense of an embattled competitor is likely to be both more profitable and more pleasant. Second, market size at any point in time is obviously the result of past growth rates. A $100 million market growing at 3 percent per year will increase to about $135 million in 10 years; the same market growing at 20 percent per year would increase to about $620 million in the same period. In addition to providing more absolute dollars of sales and profits, the larger market is likely to offer a wider variety of opportunities for investment and competitive strategies.

High industry growth does not necessarily indicate high industry profits or opportunity for any individual company, however. High-growth industries often attract strong competitors who are quite willing to sacrifice current profits in order to build a strong position in an industry that is likely to become large in a relatively short time. A prime current example would be the battle in 1982 and 1983 between Japanese and American manufacturers of the 256K RAM (random access memory) chips for use in computers. Key not only in the development and manufacture of advanced computers, leadership in this family of products is considered to be essential to overall leadership in the information technology field in the decade ahead.

As such industries mature, the leader is likely to achieve both high profits and high cash flow if the battle for market share subsides and capacity is in line with demand. Such industries can also result in a series of independent decisions by competitors that result in current capacity in excess of demand and pricing policies designed to increase or maintain market share rather than provide reasonable levels of profitability.

An industry in which capacity exceeds demand, and particularly one in which strong competitors are determined to increase market share, can be thoroughly unattractive in terms of current profits. Sometimes the periods of overcapacity seem recurring, as in the case of the insurance business and airline passenger travel. Sometimes the slumps last only a few years, as in the case of semi-conductors or pocket calculators. And sometimes the periods of over-capacity and reduced profits can last for many years, as in the case of the basic chemical industry and the fertilizer industry. The relationship of capacity to demand is likely to be a much better indicator of profitability at any given time than the growth rate of the industry.

SOURCES OF DATA

In many cases, detailed and complete industry figures abound, as for example in the case of the American automobile industry. Production and sales by manufacturer, by model, and by state are readily available and frequently reported, sometimes by weekly periods. In smaller and less mature industries or product lines, the statistics may be very difficult to come by. Sometimes production and sales figures are more readily available than profit figures; sometimes the opposite is true. In some industries you will practically be suffocated by statistics; in others you may find the lack of reliable data on market size, growth, and profitability frustrating. General managers share your difficulties and frustrations and have learned to do the best they can with the data available. You will have to strike a balance between the risk of not having important information which might be readily available with the paralysis and delay that comes from always seeking more information.

There are many sources of help that you can turn to in obtaining data about an industry or specific companies. At the industry level, the best place to start is with a general bibliography of the sources of business information, such as the excellent one by Daniels.[1] Most business libraries will have their own bibliographies of the business information that they can provide.[2] Other readily available sources include industry and company analyses from brokerage houses and the variety of company information available from the individual company.

The key question, of course, is what is likely to happen in the future, not what occurred in the past; but knowledge of what has happened to date provides the essential base for looking ahead. Industry and company statistics are but a starting point and a background for the rest of your analysis; sometimes they raise more questions than they answer. An investigation of the characteristics of the industry—such as we suggest in the next section—may help explain the performance trends of some industries and may also help you in forming judgments as to possible competitive strategies for companies within the industry.

INDUSTRY DYNAMICS

The collection of data about the industry and the competitors within it will be of little value to you until you can make it a part of your broader understanding of "how this industry works." You will want to develop an understanding of why companies in the industry behave as they do with regard to important strategic decisions affecting such items as products, pricing, and plant capacity; what influences the ways in which the companies compete with each other; and what competitive strategies seem to be available to companies in the industry. If you are studying a case about a company, your analysis will be limited to the time and data available for that purpose; if you are acting as a consultant, you may spend months on basically the same questions; and if you have made your career in the industry, understanding and keeping up with the industry and its competitors will be a continuing activity and challenge.

The field of industrial organization, a specialty within the economics profession, developed in the 1930s as a way of providing analytical support for the regulation of industry size and structure in ways thought to be conducive to more competitive corporate behavior. Proceeding from a strong early bias against large firm size and concentrated industry structures, it has come to be more concerned with explaining the behavior and economic performance of an industry in terms of the structural characteristics of the industry, including the suppliers and the customers of the industry. A recent book by Porter develops a highly structured approach to the analysis of industries based on concepts and findings from the field of industrial organization.[3]

In trying to gain an understanding of the important aspects of the way an industry works from the standpoint of a particular competitor in the industry, you should seek answers to questions in a number of broad areas.

First, what is the distribution of size of firms (or divisions of firms) with which we compete, and where do we rank? Are there many firms of somewhat equal size, or is the industry characterized by a few very large companies, with consequent large market shares, and then a large number of smaller ones? What are the strategies of firms large enough and strong enough to affect the smaller firms in the industry? Is there a single market leader which tolerates the existence of smaller firms as long as they do not try to expand too aggressively, or are there two giants battling each other for market share, using price as a competitive weapon? Endless combinations are possible, each with different implications for other firms in the industry.

Second, what economies of scale are available to firms in the industry? *Economy of scale* means simply a reduction in the costs of a unit of output that is made possible by an increase in the scale or volume of operations and the accompanying investment required. The concept of economy of scale has played a large role in both the development of theory and the empirical research of economists interested in the firm. Economies of scale are thought of as occurring most commonly in production facilities, but they can be achieved in many areas. Large companies can generally obtain both debt and equity funds more cheaply from the capital markets than can small companies; large research and development facilities for some purposes may be much more efficient than smaller ones; national advertising campaigns are cheaper in terms of unit costs than are local campaigns; expenditures for management salaries and corporate overhead generally need not increase at the same rate as sales, and so on.

Industries vary widely in the areas in which significant economies of scale, and therefore possible competitive advantage, can be achieved. It is essential for a company to select its own strategy accordingly. Companies large enough to capitalize on economies of scale with regard to their competitors will seek opportunities for doing so. Smaller firms, vulnerable to competitors able to take advantages of some scale economies (by far the more common competitive situation), will seek other ways to gain a competitive advantage.

Third, are there significant barriers to entry which either protect us or adversely affect our ability to move in other directions? A barrier to entry may be considered as the minimum ante required to enter the game or the minimum investment required to compete in the mainstream of the industry. Some industries are characterized by low barriers to entry—for example, tool and die shops serving the automotive industry, plastic injection molding manufacturers, garment manufacturers, and so on. Some have high barriers to entry, for a variety of reasons—basic steel, the integrated oil companies, and pharmaceutical companies, for example. The barriers may consist of the minimum investment required in production facilities, in the distribution system, in research and development and patents, in advertising expenditures and consumer brand identification, among other things.

Industries with low barriers to entry tend to be characterized by many small firms, relatively high turnover of firms, and often low profits; they are sometimes referred to, somewhat disparagingly, as "alley shop" or "loft" operations. Industries with high barriers to entry tend to have larger firms, a lower turnover of firms, and often higher profit margins, unless the industry also suffers from overcapacity.

Fourth, what are the characteristics and strengths of both our suppliers and customers as they affect their relationships with us? With regard to suppliers, one extreme is that of Polaroid, relying in its early years (for good reason) on Kodak as its only supplier for most of the materials needed for its instant film and performing only a few (but key) aspects of the film-manufacturing process itself. As Polaroid grew to become a half-billion-dollar competitor of the much larger Kodak by the late 60s, this became a supplier relationship that raised serious strategic questions for both Polaroid and Kodak. The other extreme of virtual independence from any one supplier is far more common, with most manufacturing companies deliberately cultivating several suppliers so as to forego the risks of being dependent on any one supplier.

Similar considerations must be given to customer relationships, where the strategic implications of relying principally on one customer are even more important than being dependent on one supplier. The stove manufacturer that sells most of its output to Sears, for example, or the tire manufacturer that has General Motors as its principal customer, will in most years have much less bargaining power than the company for whom no one customer accounts for more than a small percentage of its business. The supplier and customer relationships are partly determined by the nature of the industry but are partly a matter of choice for the firm as well. You will want to think through just what the position of your company is with regard to its supplier and customer relationships and whether the advantages of the present situation outweigh the costs of modifying those relationships.

Fifth, what is important about the financial and operating characteristics of the industry, and how are these likely to influence competitive decisions and strategies? In some industries the combination of high capital and therefore fixed costs in relation to variable costs, a production process which either must or can easily be continuous, and a largely undifferentiated product result in pressures to operate at full capacity regardless of demand, with consequent wide swings in prices and profits. The production of paper, basic chemicals, and steel would be in this category, for example. In other cases it may be the consequence of the manufacturing strategy chosen rather than the requirements of the production process that lead to high investment for high automation and consequent low unit costs at high and steady levels of throughput, leading to exactly the same kinds of pressures to maintain production regardless of market conditions. Highly automated automobile, television, or home appliance plants would be examples. A high level of forward or backward integration, with the consequent increase in assets required to support the same end sales to the consumer, is another important factor which influences both competitive behavior and profitability.

Some industries unavoidably have certain characteristics; others have competitors which have chosen to follow strategies that create certain pricing and production pressures in the industry. The building by Japanese manufacturers of highly automated and cost-efficient plants in the automobile, consumer electronics, and photographic industries—which collectively represented as much as twice the domestic consumption in those industries, for example—was a competitive strategy resulting from strategic choice, not industry necessity. The presence of such large, low-cost competitors for whom volume is essential and whose capacity far exceeds the needs of the domestic market has major implications for other companies in the industry as well as other countries, who incur deficits in their balance of trade in part because of the strategies adopted by individual companies.

You will also need to investigate what is typical in the industry for the important financial ratios: items such as amount of increased working capital and fixed assets required to support increased sales, the contribution of each incremental sales dollar to these needs, the growth rate that can be maintained from typical return on equity and dividend ratios, and so on. All of these measures have important implications with respect to the financial policies and the profit and growth goals of the individual company.

The questions and concerns suggested in the preceding five categories are by no means exhaustive. Much more could be said about the effects of technological change on industries, for example, as well as the major impact that government regulations can have on an industry. Part of the skill a general manager has to develop is the ability to think through, for each specific situation, what it is that affects in important ways the nature of competition in a given industry and what the implications are likely to be for companies in the industry.

PIMS

Two major analytical techniques have been developed which seek to provide guidance to the manager attempting to develop a strategy which takes into account a number of the factors just discussed. The first of these is the PIMS study, and the second is the notion of the experience curve.

One goal of many business practitioners as well as researchers has been to "quantify the variables that affect the profitability of a business." It is an objective disarmingly easy to state but one which has eluded the efforts of most who have tried to do so. The most ambitious attempt to accomplish this was undertaken by the General Electric Company in the early 1960s as a proprietary strategic planning technique. The effort was later transferred to the Marketing Science Institute, an independent research organization, and expanded considerably in its scope. Known as PIMS (Profit *I*mpact on Market Strategy), the project has collected data from about 800 business units supplied by 100 companies. Working with a very large number of variables, such as market share, degree of capital intensity, R&D and marketing expenditures as a percent of sales, and so on, the researchers have concluded that 37 variables can explain 80 percent of the observed variation in the profitability of the many businesses studied. Of all the variables, market share is most strongly correlated with profitability.

The application of these findings requires both considerable data and great caution, however, especially with regard to the definition of the product, relevant costs, and the market. In addition, there is the very considerable difficulty of moving from correlations of variables to conclusions about "cause" and "effect," and then for the individual company to find a way to cause the desired effect. To put the question as simply as possible, even if high market share is significantly correlated with high profits and furthermore thought to be a cause of high profits rather than a consequence of doing many things well, how can a company with low market share profitably obtain a high market share? When Philip Morris bought Miller's Brewing from the W. R. Grace Company, they set out to bring Miller's from a distant seventh or eighth in the industry to one of the volume leaders. The large increase in sales and market share was accomplished over about a decade, but only at the cost of hundreds of millions of dollars of investment and a return on investment estimated by outsiders to be marginal at best.

The findings stemming from the PIMS research suggest many interesting questions for the strategist, even though their application requires care and the approach is not without a number of strong critics. Two articles which further develop the promise of the PIMS approach are listed in footnotes 4 and 5. Two articles which raise some further cautions by pointing out, among other things, the number of companies with good profits and low market shares are noted in footnotes 6 and 7.

THE EXPERIENCE CURVE

Another approach which has gained considerable publicity within the last decade or so is that of the reduction in costs which arises as a consequence of the effects of the experience curve, as developed and popularized by the Boston Consulting Group. Simply put, it is the observation that in many cases the unit costs of production are a function of the *accumulated* production of that item, not the present level of output or capacity, and that these costs will decline (adjusted for inflation and changes in the cost of purchased goods and services) as the accumulated production of that item increases. The notion of a reduction in cost arising from accumulated experience represents a bridge between the economist's concept of economy of scale based on current absolute size and the effects of the learning curve.

Learning curves have traditionally been the province of industrial engineers and have been applied to the cost estimation and production scheduling of complex job-lot products such as airplanes and ships since World War II. The proponents of the experience curve claim that it is a much more important and pervasive phenomenon than simply the reduction in direct labor-hours that can be predicted by learning curve theory as a result of production workers becoming familiar with repetitive operations. They claim that the learning curve applies to almost all aspects in the operation of a company and that these advantages stem from accumulated experience. The advantages will be retained only by good managements, however, which use their experience to continue improving their operations to stay ahead of their competitors with less accumulated experience.

Proponents of the experience curve believe that it is essential to obtain this high market share early in the life cycle of an industry in order to have the greatest accumulated experience and therefore the lowest costs in the industry. It follows that market share leadership should be obtained at almost any cost, since it will ensure eventual high cash flow and profitability to the industry leader.

Two writings which present further the basic approach, as well as some of the limitations of the approach, are noted in footnotes 8 and 9.

APPLICATION

Just as with the PIMS approach, considerable skill and care is required in order to apply the concept and techniques of experience curve analysis to the specific situation. The definition and collection of relevant cost and market data is in itself a major undertaking for most actual situations.

Many examples can be found where aggressive production and pricing strategies based on the desire to take market leadership early and the assumption that costs will eventually decline to an acceptable proportion of prices have been successful. Henry Ford followed this strategy in the development and pricing of the Model T Ford, which by means of a low-cost position and a low price achieved a market leadership that lasted for decades; Texas Instruments is an example of a company which often has followed the same strategy in recent times in the semiconductor industry. It should be apparent, though, that if two strong companies decide to follow this basic strategy, a long and very costly battle for market share can make the battle not worth winning.

The fact that a new, large, and modern plant brought on stream by one competitor may achieve lower costs than a collection of older plants operated by another competitor, even though those old plants may represent more cumulative experience, is not addressed directly by the proponents of the experience curve. The introduction of very large breweries representing investments in the hundreds of millions of dollars, for example, represented a significant cost advantage over the many smaller, regional breweries that had characterized the industry previously.

The impact of new equipment or manufacturing technology in the hands of a competitor, regardless of the scale of the plant, is not addressed very well either. The success of a number of "mini-mills" in the steel industry, operating with a much smaller volume but a different production technology than the much larger integrated companies making up "Big Steel," would be an example of such a strategy. Most important, competitive strategies other than those based on low cost—for example, product differentiation based on special marketing expertise or product innovation—are not readily amenable to analysis by means of experience curve concepts.

In the situation where analysis stemming from the application of experience curve concepts and data leads you to recommend becoming the company with the greatest accumulated experience in whatever product the company happens to make, you will need to go on to specify a strategy which will enable you to achieve that position. The more you believe in the applicability of the experience curve, the more important it will be to achieve this position; but the more difficult it will also be to achieve if there is already someone in the industry with greater accumulated experience.

Both the PIMS approach and analysis based on experience curve concepts can suggest many interesting questions for the strategist. They also lead to a number of important hypotheses concerning the allocation of funds by the corporate level of a diversified company to the various business units comprising the company. We will examine these portfolio planning models, as they are called, in Part 3, where the focus shifts to the management of the diversified firm.

MAJOR FACTORS AFFECTING THE INDUSTRY

At some point in your analysis you will have to try to identify the major factors which affect the growth and profitability of the industry, what trends are occurring, and which of these factors are susceptible to some control. Some of these factors will be common to many industries—consumer disposable income or the level of capital goods expenditures, for example—but many will be unique to a given industry. They will encompass consumer tastes as well as finances; technical development, both within and outside the industry and country; economic trends; political developments; and social trends or pressures.

Such factors may not affect all companies or industries the same. High interest rates have a favorable effect on the demand for automobile replacement parts, for example, because new car sales are likely to suffer and consumers will fix up the cars they already own. For a mortgage banker or anyone associated with or affected by the home construction industry, however, the high interest rates (and therefore high mortgage rates) such as existed in 1979–1982 were a very strong negative factor, causing housing starts and commercial construction to decline to record lows. The extensive price controls that existed for several years in the early 1970s are another example of the many factors that can be of major importance to an industry but which can affect some industries or companies more than others. For example, the sale of large quantities of wheat to Russia at about the same time, which also resulted in unprecedented increases in the prices of domestic wheat, caused the bankruptcy of many of the smaller baking companies but was of little consequence to many other segments of the food business.

The trends that major factors are likely to take is far more important than their current level. In many cases, predicting the trends and the way they will interact with each other will be difficult and result in little consensus. Based on the trends of the past several decades, for example, a plausible case can be made that over the long term the amount of government involvement in and regulation of the economy is going to increase, that raw materials will become scarcer and more expensive, and that real wage and fringe costs per hour are likely to increase. One could also point to short-term trends directly counter to the above and argue the opposite. Similarly, one could argue that the unprecedented actual and projected budget deficits of $200 billion in the mid-80s will crowd out private investment and result in high interest rates, inflation, unemployment, or slower economic growth, or perhaps all four; and that record trade deficits of $60 to $100 billion will wreak further havoc on our economy, international relations, and world trade. But there are opposing views as to the likelihood and implications of these trends as well.

The challenge is not only to predict what these trends are likely to be and when changes will become significant, but also what the implications of them are for the individual company. Then the only task remaining will be to determine what your company can do to benefit by, rather than be harmed by, the changes that are coming.

SUMMARY

An industry can be thought of as much like the forest pond so frequently described by the naturalist—full of all sorts of animals and plants, many competing for the same limited supplies of sunlight and food, some mutually supportive, some feeding on others, some gaining in prominence or power at times, and some disappearing from the scene. In spite of the activity there is a reasonable stability and balance until some new animal comes along or some other change in the environment occurs. A company in an industry is subject to similar conditions—a variety of competitors, some larger and stronger, some with different strategies for capturing "our" sources of revenue; and unexpected disturbances from time to time in the form of changing consumer tastes, new technical developments, government regulations, economic slumps, credit restraints, raw material shortages, or foreign competition—the list is endless.

The questions you can ask and the data you can seek to help you understand the working of an industry are limited only by your own ingenuity and energy. Your objective should not be perfection in your knowledge of the industry and its environment, as that is both unattainable and unnecessary. What you need instead is sufficient information and understanding to help you proceed with confidence in analyzing and judging the opportunities and threats your company will face in the years ahead—and the strategic alternatives you will develop as a result.

You will find it very useful to try to determine which individual companies have done well in the industry and which ones have done poorly. More important, how do you explain their performance—both good and bad—and what can you learn and perhaps adopt from their experiences? Five or 10 years from now, what do you think the most succcessful companies in the industry will look like? What will be the cause of the downfall of the least successful? In view of what you learn, how can you develop a strategy that will serve your company well in the years ahead?

In order to develop recommendations for the specific company you will need to undertake a more detailed analysis of the company itself, a task to which we turn in the next chapter.

CHAPTER 5

Strategy Formulation and Corporate Resources

A corporate strategy has to be designed to fit the needs and capabilities of a specific company, not a typical company. Your strategic recommendations will need to be based not only upon your analysis of the industry but upon the problems, opportunities, resources, and aspirations of your specific company. Furthermore, the challenge is to develop a clear understanding of what the unique or distinctive competences of your company are, or can be, that will enable it to capitalize on the opportunities and minimize the threats in its competitive environment. The notion of *fit* is central to the entire process of strategy formulation. The creation of a strategy which matches corporate resources with opportunity, aspirations, and responsibilities should be your objective. This is completely different than trying to excel at everything, or simply attempting to duplicate the strengths of your competitors so that you may do battle with them on the same basis.

David attacked Goliath with a slingshot, not with brute force. In somewhat more recent times, Sloan was very explicit in his memoirs about the futility of attacking Henry Ford head-on in the early days of General Motors. As late as 1925 the Model T Ford had about 70 percent of the low-priced market, and the Ford touring car was selling for $290 versus $510 for the closest Chevrolet version. That, he commented, would be like trying to take on the U.S. Treasury. Instead, he developed a strategy that enabled Chevrolet to grow by concentrating on a slightly higher price and quality range, thereby avoiding head-on competition with Ford. Sloan hoped that the product he was offering would appeal to an increasingly large market and represent a competitive advantage as time went on because of the apparent directions in which consumer tastes and environmental trends were proceeding.

The development of better highways, the introduction of greatly improved consumer financing techniques, the acceptance of the yearly model change, the establishment of a second-hand automobile market to serve basic transportation needs, and the preference of consumers for better cars as their disposable incomes rose all contributed to the success of Sloan's strategy. In 1928, only three years later, Ford was compelled to shut down his entire production facilities for a year and a half to develop and retool for a new model, and General Motors captured a dominant position which Ford never regained. Success in this case for Sloan came not from doing what Henry Ford would have been unable to do but from assessing differently the major trends that were occurring in the environment and developing a product strategy that would benefit from those trends.[1]

Military writers have long written about the advantage of trying to engage your opponent where you are strong and he is weak, but you can be sure that an intelligent competitor is trying to gain exactly the same advantage over you. One of the objectives of your strategy should be to make it difficult for competitors to respond easily to your initiatives. A price cut, for example, is the easiest competitive move of all to respond to quickly. Unless you have a lower cost structure or stronger financial position which may benefit you in the longer term even at the lower prices, however, a price cut which others follow immediately is likely to lead to little competitive advantage. A distinctive product, a reputation for quality and service, a strong distribution network, or a strong and favorable consumer image, on the other hand, are examples of competitive advantages or areas of distinctive competence that are not so easy to attack.

In this chapter we would like to give you some suggestions that will help you in identifying the present position of the company, evaluating that position in view of the conditions and trends in the industry, and developing some strategic recommendations based on industry and company economic factors that you feel are appropriate to the situation. We have not yet discussed the values and aspirations of the management or the expectations of society as they affect the determination of strategy, and you will need to consider these before proposing changes in strategy for the company. We will discuss these areas in more detail in the next chapters. At this point we will turn our attention from the focus of the last chapter, that of understanding the external world as it affects the company, to the internal world of the company itself and its position in its environment.

PRESENT POSITION

Your first task is to gain an understanding of what the company is, how it works, what its strategy is, and what may be major problems or opportunities. You need to emphasize the development of relevant facts before the development of firm conclusions at this point, in spite of the need to form some tentative conclusions early in your analysis in order to direct your attention to data and issues that may be important. The ability to make such a broad evaluation or size-up of a company is a key skill of the successful general manager.

The skills required to evaluate a company are not unlike the diagnostic skills possessed by the experienced medical doctor. In both business and medicine there are many measures or symptoms one could look at, but only some will turn out to be important. Furthermore, it is usually the collection of performance measures or symptoms that is necessary for the successful diagnosis of a business or a patient, seldom just isolated measures. That careful, quantitative analysis can be applied to specific measures or symptoms should not obscure the need for skill, judgment, and experience to observe and select what is important to investigate more thoroughly. This is an activity that experienced executives are often much better at than students, just as the experienced doctor is likely to be much better at making preliminary diagnoses than the intern in residency. That is one reason interns go through a period of residency during which they accompany experienced doctors as they make their rounds.

You can achieve similar results, although probably not as quickly as a manager familiar with performance analysis, through the thoughtful analysis of selected portions of the data present in cases or available for the company you are interested in. A less useful approach, in our view, is the mechanical manipulation of all of the available data, devoting equal attention to all areas. Whenever you undertake an evaluation of a company you should attempt to make educated guesses as soon as possible as to the areas most worthy of investigation, and then pursue them. They will not all turn out to be fruitful, but we believe it will be more useful and educational for you to focus your attention on a series of areas in this manner rather than routinely complete a checklist.

As much as we would like to discourage you from the mechanical use of a checklist, however, we would like to suggest that there are a number of major areas you will invariably want to at least skim, if the information is available, to see if there appear to be grounds for more detailed investigation.

FINANCIAL ANALYSIS

Your first step in any strategic evaluation of a company should be to examine the financial information available for whatever leads it may provide with regard to present or potential problem areas or constraints. Many of your strategic recommendations are likely to require the expenditure of money, and recommendations arrived at without attention to the problem of financing them are likely to be of little value. Even more important, you will not find it easy to justify recommendations which do not take account of a current financial crisis, no matter how admirable those recommendations might be for the longer term.

Much information can be obtained from the profit and loss statements for clues as to what is happening to the business. What is the level of, and trend in, dollar profits, earnings per share, return on equity, costs, and margins? How do they compare with industry figures, with the recent past for the company, and with the plans, if they are available?

A similar investigation of the balance sheet is appropriate. You will particularly want to check the level of and trends in the current ratio, working capital, and the debt/capitalization ratio to see if the firm appears to be in or headed for short-term financial difficulties. Ratios and levels of inventories and receivables are always important to check. So are upcoming large outlays for debt repayment or capital expenditures in order to be sure the funds required will be available. Lenders tend to concentrate on balance sheet ratios and coverage ratios, the extent to which earnings or cash flow cover interest payments, and debt repayment provisions.

A number of important ratios depend upon information from both the balance sheet and the profit and loss statements, as with some of the items mentioned above. One important figure to compute is the rate of growth that the firm can sustain from internal sources, which is roughly equal to the ratio of the profits remaining after payment of taxes and dividends divided by the net worth of the company. This assumes that all of the expansion of the equity base will come from internally generated profits, and that debt will be added to the capital structure as needed to maintain the same levels of debt to equity. If increased debt is possible or if the sale of equity is not ruled out, the growth that can be financed is of course greater; but the sustainable growth rate (SGR) from internal sources is a very useful measure to be aware of when evaluating the growth plans of a company. If a company plans to grow at 15 percent a year but has a SGR of 8 percent, a management which does not want to issue more equity (for whatever reasons), and a debt ratio which is already at a prudent maximum, financing the growth will be interesting indeed.

It may be useful for you to remember that various groups may look at somewhat different measures within the company, depending upon the interest they have in that company. Lenders will tend to look at measures that affect the security of their loans to the company. Investors will be more concerned with dividends, returns being earned on their equity, and factors that will influence the price of the common stock. Managers have to pay a great deal of attention to measures that reflect the operating position of the company but also need to pay careful attention to the viewpoints of both lenders and investors.

The possible number of items and ratios to look at is large, but as you gain experience you will develop an ability to skim a large number of items efficiently, focusing on those which may, in combination with other bits of information, signal problems. Trends and, especially, sudden changes are generally more important than current figures alone; and almost all figures or ratios will take on more meaning if there is a basis of comparison available with other companies, industry figures, and the history of the company itself. Some of the most important and perceptive analyses can consist of simple arithmetic and the combination of data from various sources, and not the sophisticated but mechanical manipulation of large amounts of data which can so easily give one the illusion of thoroughness, precision, and progress.

An excellent reference with much more detailed definitions of various financial ratios and their method of computation is *Techniques of Financial Analysis* by Helfert, and especially Chapter 2.[2] Many sources of information concerning industry trends are available from both specific industry magazines and associations and from more general sources. A comprehensive and up-to-date source for financial ratios for a large number of companies and industries is the periodic "Key Business Indicators" found in *Dun's Review*.[3]

FACILITIES, PRODUCTS, AND MARKETS

There is a temptation to spend too much time on the analysis of financial performance and position as described above and not enough time on the more difficult analysis of the underlying factors that have led to that performance. The numbers are largely a result of the combination of the facilities, the products, and the marketing efforts of the company. They are a representation of the reality, however, and not the reality. If you want to influence the numbers you will have to influence the reality, just as you must treat the patient who has the fever, not the thermometer that indicates a fever.

In evaluating the position of a company you would be greatly remiss in concentrating on the more readily available financial statistics at the expense of seeking information about and making judgments on the more difficult business areas mentioned above. You should make the best possible evaluation you can with the data available of the physical facilities of the company with regard to age and efficiency as well as capacity to serve the projected demands to be placed upon them; the principal products, their technology, and the state of the research and development efforts supporting them; and the position and reputation of these products in the market, as well as the marketing and service organization itself. Quantitative data may be available and useful for some of these items; qualitative assessments will have to suffice for many.

You should try to determine if there are major efforts or crises occurring within the company. Do some of these areas represent areas of competitive vulnerability or, more happily, possible competitive advantages? Is the company undergoing a transition in several of these areas at once, which may cause unusual difficulties? Small but successful companies, for example, usually find it necessary at some stage in their growth to change from an entrepreneurial to a more professional management style. The development of a new generation of products, which in turn may require new or greatly expanded plant facilities and more people, is also likely to occur at some time. If both of these changes should occur at the same time that the company needs to develop significant sources of new financing, the demands on management time and skills will be great. Each of these transitions can pose a significant but surmountable challenge all by itself; occurring together, they may provide too much for most managements. Similar constellations of problems in various areas, each one quite manageable in itself, can overtake any company.

You should do your best to determine—by product line or major line of business, if possible—where the assets of the company are invested; profits in relation to assets by product lines; and what may be expected by product line in terms of sales, profits, and requirements of assets and people. Almost every company can break down its products or services into categories with different production requirements or performance characteristics. Before making recommendations to the company you will want to ascertain, as best you can, just where the company has committed, or plans to commit, its assets, and what their important sources of profits are.

HUMAN RESOURCES

How many times have you seen or heard a company state "People are our most important asset"? Regardless of the extent to which actions follow words with regard to these sentiments, an essential part of the evaluation of any company is an evaluation of the quality, competence, and dedication of the people of which it is comprised. Part of that evaluation can certainly be based on the record of the company and separate portions of it, but part of the evaluation will have to be based on a myriad of other observations.

Some companies may have strengths in certain areas and not in others, such as a strong research and development department but average or worse marketing personnel. Other companies may have departments that are neither weak nor strong in relation to industry standards, but they nevertheless function together very effectively. In any company the quality of the work force may be just as important as the quality of management, and both must be evaluated if you are to make judgments about the relative strengths of one company to another.

There is a great temptation to evaluate management on the basis of past performance, largely because it is so difficult to find an analytical and objective basis for making evaluations independent cf the past. It should be apparent, though, that quite often managements deserve less credit than they claim when things go well and less blame than they receive when things go poorly. There is much that intervenes between the competence and efforts of management and the results that occur that are beyond the control of the management.

You will have to make some judgments about how much to allow for these intervening factors in assessing the competence of a management to deal with the problems and opportunities of the future. It may be of some comfort to you, as you unavoidably wrestle with these judgments, to know that a major bond rating service made a serious attempt to develop a way to rate managements as a part of a proposed new service. After considerable discussion and investigation, they concluded that such a thing was not yet possible to do with confidence in a routine and reproducible way. Of all the areas in which you must make judgments, the one concerned with the quality and competence of managers is the least amenable to quantification or a precise protocol and the most dependent on experience and personal skills.

SUMMARY

Deciding just what the distinctive strengths *and* weaknesses of the organization are is one of the important tasks you will have to accomplish as a general manager as you deal with the problem of formulating a strategy for the company. Such an evaluation is both an intellectual and emotional challenge, and disseminating and acting upon that determination is likely to be a significant administrative challenge as well. It is much like trying to be in a parade and on the reviewing stand at the same time. You will no doubt find the task easier from the more detached viewpoint of a student than the involved role of the general manager assessing his own company and colleagues (and himself!), but the former is merely practice for the latter. The task becomes harder, not easier.

Although it is satisfying to try to identify those aspects in which a company has a distinct advantage over its competitors, it is far less rewarding to identify those areas in which the company is at a distinct disadvantage, especially if the areas concern people currently a part of the organization. It is even more difficult for a subordinate to suggest such areas of weakness. In altogether too many organizations such statements are interpreted as indicating disloyalty, lack of team spirit, or lack of understanding and true appreciation of the "fine qualities that made this company great." And in the case of making unfavorable judgments about people, this is hardly a way to make friends.

Such judgments need to be made by someone, however, because a strategy which is not based on an awareness of the strengths and weaknesses of a company relative to its competitors can very easily lead to difficulties. An evaluation of the financial performance and position of the company is but one part of that task—and the part for which the data are most readily available and the form of analysis most readily taught.

Superior results come from outperforming your competitors in one or more tasks, or combination of tasks, that contribute to success—having lower manufacturing costs, more effective advertising, better R&D, a stronger distribution system, better overall coordination, a superior product strategy, or whatever. The fact is, however, that every company in an industry does *not* offer the best quality or the highest value; is *not* the leader in product development; does *not* have the lowest-cost manufacturing facilities, and so on. Strategies which are not built on the actual corporate resources and distinctive competences are not likely to be successful. Neither are strategies which blindly attack competitors on their strong points.

As you progress through your analysis, you should now be coming to the point where you feel more confident of proposing some tentative strategic recommendations that will take into account your investigation of the industry, your evaluation of the present position and problems of the company, and the distinctive strengths on which the company may build. Applying the same form of analysis to your competitors will help you anticipate what their options and responses are likely to be, an essential factor to take into account in your own strategy formulation process. We will turn next to a consideration of what the management *wants* to do, not only what they *might* do on the basis of industry opportunity and company competences.

CHAPTER 6

Strategy Formulation and Management Values

We have thus far discussed strategy formulation as a matching of opportunities and threats in the environment with the strengths and weaknesses of the company itself to achieve economic goals. A strategy based on such factors may be called an *economic* strategy, even though it takes into account far more than just the economic aspects of the environment of the company. It is economic in the sense that it presumes the objectives of the management are overwhelmingly economic in nature. The process is commonly thought of as one which should be objective and rational, although with ample room for different conclusions based on different judgments about critical factors affecting the strategy. The process is complex, but nonetheless the product of reasoned analysis by managers who are assumed not to let their own values interfere with their professional analysis any more than medical doctors would let their personal values influence their diagnosis or treatment of a patient. Although strategies may differ, the goal is presumed to be long-term profit maximization within the law, largely uninfluenced by the personal preferences of the managers involved.

It is of course useful to simplify reality for purposes of both teaching and research. We cannot talk about everything at once, and it makes little sense to talk about the impact of the values of management on the strategy of the company until we have discussed the economic factors both inside and outside of the company that influence that strategy strongly.

In addition, there are considerable advantages to making the assumption that firms are—or at least should be—primarily economic units, all seeking the common goals of maximizing the long-run return on the common stockholders' equity in a rational and analytical manner. It has simplified greatly the development of normative economic models of firms and industries and their ideal role in the wider national economy; and it has provided a framework for the development of numerous analytical models useful for decision making within the firm.

The everyday observations of all of us, however, should be sufficient reminder that the personal values of those with power within the organization have an influence on the longer-term objectives, the strategies, and the everyday working environment of the organization. In order to understand the strategy of a company, why the company has evolved as it has, as well as what kinds of recommendations might be acceptable to the management, it is essential to think about the values of the managers involved. What kinds of people are they? What are the backgrounds of the key executives, and how have those backgrounds influenced them? How have the beliefs and assumptions they hold influenced the company? How much would your possible strategic recommendations run counter to these, and how strong would your case have to be to convince them to change to accommodate your suggestions? And why, if the influence of their personal values is critical in a decision you think should come out differently, are your personal values better than theirs?

The issue is not only the degree to which you will be able to influence the managers you work with, but also the degree to which you will recognize how much your personal values affect your own decisions. You will have to decide the extent to which you should let your values influence your decisions.

The distinction between personal values and a belief in specific forms of corporate responsibility, both of which affect management decisions, is not precise. Happily, it need not be. For some, the desire to use corporate resources to help society achieve goals which can only remotely be justified as being in the economic interests of that company's shareholders in the foreseeable future is a strongly held personal value. We will discuss the concept of corporate responsibility in Chapter 7. In this chapter we will focus more on the impact of a variety of personal values on the strategy, the people, and the everyday operations of the organization.

VALUES AND STRATEGY

Evidence of the impact of personal values on the character of a business is widespread but perhaps more apparent in small companies. As you observe or read about or study any new or small company dominated largely by one man, for example, try to determine what role the background and values of the founder have played in the development of that company. What limitations might they place on recommendations based only on an economic analysis of the company, its problems, and its opportunities? Attitudes with regard to acceptable or desirable levels of growth, profitability, risk, and personal control differ widely, and they affect the character of the business in fundamental ways.

The Leisure Group, Inc., a company that achieved some prominence in the financial community in the late 60s and early 70s because of its impressive financial performance and consequent high price-earnings multiple, is an example of a company that was influenced strongly by the high growth aspirations of its managers and their tolerance for a large degree of personal and corporate risk.

In that case two young entrepreneurs with impressive educational and work backgrounds were able to borrow, on the basis of an investment of only $8,000 of their own, another $550,000 for the purpose of buying companies in the "leisure industry." Within six years they had achieved sales of $58 million and a net worth of about $31 million by means of an aggressive acquisition program and extensive restructuring of the companies they bought, all the while operating with a highly leveraged financial position. In the seventh year they unfortunately lost $31 million as well as a great many friends in the financial community. Their enthusiasm for growth continued undiminished, however, in spite of continuing losses, a negative net worth, and the unhappiness of their lenders, who now controlled the company.

The values of management affect far more than just decisions concerning the degree of risk that is acceptable in pursuing the traditional goals of growth and profits. Jay Monroe, the outspoken president of the Tensor Corporation, a manufacturer of high-intensity lamps and metal tennis racquets, was very explicit about (1) his lack of interest in projects undertaken only because they might be profitable, (2) his scorn for the "MBA" type of analysis, (3) his practice of undertaking activities only if they were of interest to him, and (4) his unabashed interest in maintaining control of the company. As he once stated in an interview, he was much concerned with the issue of maintaining control of the company because he liked his job and "No independent selection of a president would result in me." He was quite proud of following what he considered much higher and broader goals than just earning a return for the stockholders of his publicly held company in the traditional way.

Edwin Land of Polaroid is a more recent and better-known example of how the values of one man can influence a company strongly. Edwin Land founded Polaroid in 1934 but did not become committed to instant photography until after World War II. From the time of the introduction of the first instant camera and film in 1948, however, Land made it clear to all that the primary business of Polaroid was, and was to remain for the foreseeable future, instant photography. That strategy, combined with a highly distinctive product and extensive patent protection, brought great success to Polaroid.

The dominance of Land, admired during the periods of Polaroid's great success, came under attack in the late 70s and early 80s. When Polaroid, by that time approaching $1.5 billion in sales, suffered a series of product and financial setbacks, the company was widely criticized for not having diversified into fields other than instant photography. Land remained adamant in his commitment to instant photography as a field in its infancy, not maturity, and to the concept of Polaroid as a research-based company concentrating the bulk of its resources on instant photography. He continued to insist that

> the role of industry is to sense a deep human need. Any market already existing is inherently boring and dull . . . The majority of our resources are going into instant photography, and that is an official statement.[1]

The issue is not whether Land's position was "right" or "wrong" from a purely economic point of view. One can easily argue that his dominance had much to do with the outstanding success of the company during its first 30 years as well as something to do with its later difficulties. The important point for our purposes is to recognize the extent to which strongly held values of managers can influence the strategy of the company in important ways. How to understand and influence the behavior of managers on matters they feel strongly about are important questions that you will have to learn to deal with in your study of cases and in your own career.

VALUES AND THE ORGANIZATION

The values of the manager can strongly affect not only the strategy of the company but also the character of the organization and the working environment of all its members. In the Midway Foods Corporation, for example, a widely studied case dealing with the job of the general manager, the influence of the owner-president on the criteria to be applied in a promotion decision involving a middle-level manager in the small, privately held company is both clear and controversial.[2]

The manager being considered for promotion is a pro-segregationist; the president is a liberal and a long-time anti-segregationist. The president agrees that the issue is not competence to do the job or management potential, but the person's views on segregation, which are fundamentally different than the strongly held personal views of the president. Would you advise the president to ignore such extraneous factors? Would you accept his reservations and perhaps opposition as regretable but understandable in view of the fact that he owns the company? Would you compliment him for using the power of his position as president to take a stand thought by many, but not all, to be morally preferable to the views of his subordinate? Or would you approve of his stand on purely economic grounds for the reason that any executive team has to be made up of members with similar values in order to work together effectively and to make promotions which may make that team less effective is simply poor management? If you should decide to support the president in this matter, would you tell the person who is not going to be promoted that the reason is the president does not like his personal views on segregation, even though they would not affect his ability to do the job for which he is being considered? And finally, to what degree should the law address questions such as this?

The issue of the criteria to be applied to the selection and promotion of people within the organization is surely one of the most important tasks of the general manager. Consider, for example, the following quote from an outstanding classic on management, *The Functions of the Executive* by Chester Barnard, who at the time of writing (1938) had long experience as president of the New Jersey Bell Telephone Company:

> ### Fitness
> In all the good organizations I have observed the most careful attention is paid to it (the informal executive organization) . . . The general method of maintaining an informal executive organization is to operate and to select and promote executives so that a general condition of compatibility of personnel is maintained. Perhaps often and certainly occasionally men cannot be promoted or selected, or even must be relieved, because they cannot function, because they "do not fit," where there is no question of formal competence. This question of "fitness" involves such matters as education, experience, age, sex, personal distinctions, prestige, race, nationality, faith, politics, sectional antecedents; and such very specific personal traits as manners, speech, personal appearance, etc. It goes by few if any rules . . . It represents in its best sense the political aspects of personal relationship in formal organization . . . it is certainly of major importance in all organization.[3]

Do these observations seem accurate to you in terms of the factors important currently in gaining membership in "the informal executive organization"? If you attempt to make the very important distinction between the "what is" and the "what should be" in the world, the extent to which his observations describe the reality, if not your ideal, in the organization you are working for or seeking to understand is surely important. You may also want to think about the extent to which such factors *should* be taken into account, and whether the type or size of the organization affect greatly your ideal or actual practice. Would your ideal or actual practice be different, for example, depending on whether the business is large or small, privately or publicly owned? Even more broadly, to what extent do his observations, if relevant, apply equally well to military, religious, governmental, and educational organizations?

WHAT ARE THE DESIRABLE LIMITS?

The Leisure Group, Tensor, Polaroid, Midway, and Barnard examples are only a few of the many that could be presented to illustrate the influence of the personal values of management on both the strategy and the everyday operations of the firm. They also raise the question of the degree of influence by the manager that

1. Is wise from the standpoint of contributing to the overall objectives of the firm.
2. Is fair to those affected by the decisions.
3. Is acceptable in view of your own values.
4. Is consistent with the goals that the broader society deems desirable for business at that particular time.

In view of the current prohibitions against discrimination in employment based on race, sex, religion, color, or national origin, for example, it is highly unlikely that any executive would write or speak as Barnard did some 40 years ago. An interesting recent case on these issues involving the prestigious New York law firm of Cravath, Swaine & Moore illustrates the extent to which decisions formerly thought to be private are increasingly subject to law and the inevitable litigation which follows. The plaintiff charged Cravath with violating Title VII of the Civil Rights Act of 1964 for allegedly denying him partnership in the firm because he was a Catholic and of Italian heritage. In addition, a survey of the 20 largest law firms in New York City revealed that of the 912 partners listed, only 15 had Italian surnames, and only 62 had graduated from Catholic law schools.

Cravath denied the charges but also argued that the law did not apply to partnership selections and that interference in the partnership selection process would violate the firm's First Amendment right of association. As part of the case for the plaintiff, it was argued that law firms, even though partnerships, certainly are businesses as they provide employment to their members, profits to their owners, and offer their services to the public for a fee.

Selection on the basis of some of the factors mentioned by Barnard is necessary to the efficient functioning of any purposive organization. The factors which should be taken into account, the degree to which they should influence managerial decisions, the remedy to be applied in cases where you think the influence inappropriate, and the way in which you will let your own personal values in these matters influence your decisions when you are in a position of responsibility are issues to be explored. The development of highly detailed laws specifying what "equal employment opportunity" consists of and the increasing trend to apply these standards to all levels within the organization is ample evidence that decisions formerly considered to be a private matter will be increasingly subject to public scrutiny and influence.

IMPACT ON THE MANAGER

The relationship between the personal values of the manager and the strategy and operations of the company can result in a significant impact on the manager as well as on the company. This is clearly demonstrated, for example, by the resignation in 1977 of the president of Holiday Inns, Inc., a company with revenues of $1.3 billion.

It was reported in *The Wall Street Journal* that when the company approved its first venture into casino gambling—a proposal to build and operate a $55 million hotel-casino in Atlantic City, New Jersey—Mr. Clymer, the president, chose to take early retirement. A company executive stated the board felt that it was simply a prudent business decision, and that hotel casinos were a logical extension of their current business. Mr. Clymer, who had long opposed casino gambling in the company's hotels, said that personal and religious reasons prompted him to ask for early retirement. "This is a personal conviction not involving the financial or business aspects of the industry," he stated. "The great concern in my heart is that some may erroneously read into this action a silent judgment of those who have reached a different conclusion. . . . This most certainly isn't the case."[4]

That Mr. Clymer's decision was a wise one for him seems to be illustrated by the events of several years later. In October 1981, Holiday Inns received some unfavorable publicity as a result of a New Jersey attorney general's report prepared as part of an examination of the suitability of Holiday Inns as a casino operator in Atlantic City. The report charged both Holiday Inns and its Harrah's gambling subsidiary in Nevada (purchased in 1980 for $300 million) with a number of practices that would adversely affect their application to construct and operate a gambling casino in Atlantic City. Earlier New Jersey state reports on Resorts International, Caesar's World, Inc., and Bally Manufacturing Corporation had also raised issues against the firms, but all three ultimately were granted licenses. Two of the firms had to agree to remove their chairmen in the process and were challenging that awkward provision in state and federal courts.

A spokesman for Holiday Inns denied that the firm or its Harrah's subsidiary had been involved in wrongdoing and predicted the commission would grant a permanent license. Regardless of the merits or outcome of the case, it is clear that Holiday Inns was involved in a new type of business activity that executives of an earlier era might not feel comfortable with. You are likely to face similar choices at some time in your career, starting with your choice of an employer and an industry.

PERSONAL GUIDELINES

In learning to deal effectively with the values of the management in the organization in which you work, you should attempt to:

1. Recognize, as best you can, the extent to which certain practices or decisions are, or have been, influenced by the personal values of someone in a position of power and responsibility.

2. Assess how important these practices or decisions are with regard to the economic well-being of the company. Hopefully most will be designed to have a positive influence, but some may be negative.

3. Come to some judgment about the appropriateness of the values themselves and the degree to which the manager has let personal values, quite apart from economic considerations, affect professional decisions.

4. Structure and present your recommendations so that a person in power, who may have quite different values than you do, will nevertheless be moved to action along the lines you recommend.

Management, of course, does not own the corporation. The law is clear on the responsibilities of management to manage the company within the law and in the interests of the shareholders, which has uniformly been interpreted to be the pursuit of primarily economic objectives. Management does, however, have very considerable leeway in practice with regard to how it shall seek these economic objectives. To assist you in developing some standards by which you might judge the appropriateness of your own personal values as well as those of others on decisions affecting the corporation, we would like to suggest the following questions:

1. Have you allowed for a reasonable input from others in the organization and from the groups or individuals that might be affected by your decision?

2. Would you be willing to acknowledge publicly both your beliefs and the extent to which they have influenced your decision?

3. Do you honestly feel that your decisions or actions are fair to the groups involved according to reasonably accepted standards of fairness? Would you object to being treated in that way yourself?

SUMMARY

We raise the issue of the impact of the personal values and aspirations of the management on both the strategy and the implementation of that strategy because our concern is with the administration of real enterprises involving real people, with all of the complications that entails. The values of the managers on a variety of dimensions—standards of integrity, ways of doing business, growth and profit goals, acceptable levels of risk, criteria for hiring and promotion, and so on—exert an influence in all organizations. These influences will have an effect on the attainment of purely economic goals, but they will also have an effect on all those who work for or have some dealings with the company.

The personal values of those in a position of influence are important in all types of organized activity—law firms, the government, the military, labor, and religious organizations. In every era there are strong and well-known leaders whose personalities dominate their organizations. Men such as Walter Reuther and James Hoffa of the labor movement and General Curtis LeMay and Admiral Hyman Rickover of the military are but a few that come to mind. The individual heads of state that have cast a strong personal imprint on their parties and governments while they are in power are too numerous to mention.

The impact of the personal values of the manager may seem more visible and important to us in small companies than in large companies. The influence exists in companies of all sizes, however, as should be apparent from the much-publicized impact of the personal style and values of such executives as Alfred P. Sloan, Jr., on General Motors, Thomas Watson on IBM, Harold Geneen on IT&T, and Edwin Land on Polaroid. Indeed, there is persuasive evidence in recent books such as *In Search of Excellence*[5] and *Corporate Cultures*[6] that a significant part of the success of many of our outstanding companies can be attributed to the impact of the strong personal values of their founders not only on the products and ways of doing business, but on the overall culture of the company.

The personal values of the manager can influence the company in many ways. We can only judge the values of others in relation to our own standards or the expectations of the broader society, however. We shall deal in the next chapter with the issues of what society, or vocal segments of society, expect of businesses in addition to the traditional role of providing employment, goods and services, and a return to the suppliers of capital.

Strategy Formulation and Corporate Responsibility

The fourth major influence on the formulation of corporate strategy that you should take into account is that of corporate responsibility.

The concept of corporate responsibility is not well defined, either in theory or in practice. The terms *social responsibility* or *public expectations* are sometimes used as well, and we will take these all to signify an important area of concern for the manager interested both in the economic well-being of his company and the role that it plays in the broader society.

It is of course a prime responsibility of the leader of an organization to see to it that the organization obeys the law. The concept of corporate responsibility is most often and most usefully applied to actions not specifically covered by law, however, where the issue is not legality but the choices available within the law. Illegal behavior is irresponsible, but not all legal behavior is *responsible* in the sense the term is commonly used.

It is apparent that business firms are increasingly being held responsible for far more than simply obeying present laws in the pursuit of economic goals for their shareholders. Because of the overwhelming importance in nonsocialist countries of the role of private enterprise in the furnishing of employment and the utilization of productive assets to provide goods and services, society has a legitimate interest in the manner in which these activities are carried out.

We will use the term *corporate responsibility*, then, to cover the activities of the corporation that are seen by others as having a sufficient economic or social impact on the broader society, or segments of it, to justify the use of outside influence, ultimately law or regulation, to affect these decisions. The influence may come via the traditional legal attempts to place resolutions on the proxy statements for vote at annual stockholders' meetings. It can also be exerted very effectively by means of the many other ways of persuasion, publicity, and pressure open in a free society to individuals and groups with a cause. The argument for change often rests on moral grounds, but the most effective pressure for change often consists of potential or actual economic harm to the firm. Ultimately, change may be compelled via law and regulation if those espousing the cause can muster the political power to achieve their goals through legislative channels.

The issue of corporate responsibility actually breaks down into two basic questions: the *legitimacy* of the power held by corporate executives and the *proper exercise* of that power. Questions concerning the legitimacy of the power derive from the fact that executives are neither selected by nor accountable to the broader community, even though their actions affect that community significantly. We will turn to this issue later in the chapter.

The proper exercise of the power held, totally apart from the means by which that power is achieved, is perhaps the more common concern of those seeking to influence the corporation. If one is dissatisfied with the actual decisions made, however, it is of course natural to attack the legitimacy of the power to make those decisions as well. As a result, the issues of legitimacy of power and the responsible exercise of that power often become intertwined in practice.

The broad question you will have to answer will be *"To whom am I responsible and for what?"* As a general manager you will have very substantial influence over factors affecting the everyday lives of many people. The exercise of the power cannot be avoided; decisions have to be made continuously on a variety of issues which affect both the economic performance of the firm and the interests of a large number of people both inside and outside the firm.

There have been some attempts to categorize the groups affected by the corporation's decisions as "stakeholders" (in addition to the traditional shareholders): employees, the local community, minorities, suppliers, customers, and so on. The purpose of such a classification is to facilitate identifying the impact of the corporation's decisions on various stakeholders as well as to explore means by which the various groups affected by the corporation's actions can gain a voice in the decisions.

In recent years, for example, partly as a consequence of the greatly increased number of unfriendly takeovers and the closing of plants that occurs during difficult economic times, there has been considerable discussion of the need to give more voice to the employees of the company in decisions affecting their future. The social justice as well as the economic efficiency of a legal system which grants the sole authority for long-term and irreversible decisions to shareholders who may have bought their shares yesterday and could sell them tomorrow is increasingly being questioned. The power of shareholders to force mergers and of managements to close plants is uniquely American; in most other developed countries, law and practice are both much more restrictive. A recent provocative proposal to change our present form of corporate governance to obtain a different balance in the rights of stockholders, management, and employees while still promoting economic efficiency involves federal rather than state chartering of corporations and a significant change in the composition of the boards of directors and the rights of shareholders, and illustrates well the complexities involved in changing our present methods of corporate governance.[1]

CATEGORIES OF RESPONSIBILITY

It may be useful to think of the many types of claims on and criticism of the corporation that come under the broad heading of corporate responsibility as falling into five rough categories:

1. Those items which are largely a consequence of the manufacturing process itself. Emissions into the atmosphere and discharges into the waterways from our steel, oil, chemical, and paper industries would be but a few examples of industries that have had to make major changes in their traditional manufacturing technologies in order to comply with evolving knowledge and regulations. The nuclear industry is another example of a technology with extremely serious consequences for society if the manufacturing processes are not designed and managed properly. Many of our most difficult pollution problems are in this category, as are worker health and safety conditions related to the job.

2. Those items related to the sale and use of the product, which can also include pollution and safety aspects, as in the case of automobiles. It would also include products with predictable adverse effects to the user, at least on a statistical basis, such as liquor and tobacco. Injury arising from accidents and even the improper use of the product, ranging from injury from chain saws to an infant choking on a button from a stuffed animal, are also in this category.

3. Company policies in such areas as hiring, promotion, termination, vacation, medical, insurance, and retirement benefits and practices. These often affect primarily the existing employees; but some of these practices are increasingly being viewed as matters for external regulation rather than items to be resolved in the process of bargaining over conditions of employment at the time of periodic labor negotiations. Lawsuits over grounds for termination and over alleged age discrimination in hiring and promotion, for example, have become much more common in recent years.

4. Actions a company can take which would affect individuals largely outside of the company and which are independent of the nature of the product or its manufacture. Examples would include building or closing plants; the hiring, training, and promotion of the disadvantaged (although this can clearly affect existing employees as well); contributions of money and/or time to charitable or educational activities; and participation in urban rehabilitation programs.

5. Actions in which the ethical practices, and not necessarily the results of the practices, are the primary concern: management compensation and employment contracts, policies on expense accounts and entertainment, bribes and illegal contributions, deceptive marketing practices, investment in undesirable activities or areas, and so on.

The above is, of course, only a partial list; you may wish to add items that you think should be on it or items that it is apparent others feel are a responsibility of the corporation. Neither are the categories mutually exclusive; many items can be placed in several categories. The categories do tend to present different kinds of problems and opportunities from the viewpoint of the manager, however; and we will look later at some specific examples of issues that have been much in the news in the last several years.

EXERCISE OF POWER

We will turn next to the question of what is a "proper exercise" of the power you will have as a general manager. Unfortunately, there is little in the way of theory to provide you with guidance for the above question. Both legal and economic theory state in essence that "The Social Responsibility of Business Is to Increase Its Profits," as Milton Friedman has argued so well in an article with the above title.[2] Most of us, however, would regard that as less than we personally would like to see companies do. It is less than almost all segments of society expect of companies. It is also less than might be wise for companies to undertake on their own, long before the public brings pressure to bear, in order to minimize the chances of legislation and regulation which could have been avoided by means of foresight on the part of management.

The dilemma, of course, is that the possible claims are endless, the resources and skills are limited, and neither the theory for what should be undertaken nor the mechanism by which conflicts can be resolved are clear. To complicate the matter further, managers do have a responsibility for the health and survival of the firm in purely economic terms, and pursuing those goals in most companies can fully occupy the manager's time and abilities. Indeed, in the economist's ideal world of perfect competition, no manager or company would have the excess resources or time to pursue anything other than profit maximization under the law. Issues of corporate responsibility would not exist. It is apparent, however, that the more business is perceived as pursuing that classical goal, the more it is subject to criticism from those who expect it to do more for society.

The range of issues for which business has been criticized either for not doing enough or for doing the wrong thing is long. Not all claims and complaints can be heeded. Neither, for reasons of both wisdom and morality, can all be ignored. Demands for preferences to minorities in hiring beyond what is specified in the law and requests for contributions to local charities both ask of the corporation that it do something it is not required to do and which it might find difficult to justify purely in terms of its own short-term economic interests. Improving opportunities for the disadvantaged or supporting various community charitable organizations may both benefit the company in the long run, but those can also be argued as the proper concern of the broader community, not individual segments of it. You will have to decide how the limited resources of the corporation are to be distributed among such competing claims. The issue is to decide what could and should be done about such claims.

A CONTROVERSIAL PRODUCT

To help you develop guidelines and an approach where so little theory or accepted rationale exists, it might be useful to consider some typical issues that have been much in the news in recent years. Consider, for example, these comments of Mr. William Ruger, the founder, president, and substantial stockholder of a company with about $20 million in sales:

> I think it's a perfect picture of a model company. It has made money honestly, provided for its employees, advanced the technology of the industry, and continued to grow and be profitable. . . . I like my job and am proud of what I'm doing. I'm proud of this company.[3]

The principal business of the above company is the design, manufacture, and distribution of high-quality handguns, and the company is indeed well-managed and an acknowledged leader in its field. In view of the problems caused by the widespread ownership of handguns in the United States, is there justification for considering this company and therefore its president to be irresponsible with regard to the occasional tragic consequences of the widespread possession of its products, or products like them supplied by other manufacturers?

Ownership of handguns in the United States on both an absolute and per capita basis far exceeds that of any other country. Our rate of homicide by means of guns is the highest in the world. Public opinion polls almost always support more restrictions on handguns, often by a wide margin, and especially in and around the larger urban centers of the country. Law enforcement officials are generally much in favor of stricter controls.

The ease with which handguns and other weapons can be purchased in the United States is commented on frequently. A recent article describing the increasing traffic in weapons in Florida noted that "customers in local gun shops can browse among arms ranging from sawed-off shotguns through an array of easily concealable handguns to well-known submachine guns."[4] Restrictions seem to be largely ineffective in limiting the sale or screening the purchasers of a wide variety of weapons.

Opposition to increased controls over handguns has been very effectively voiced by various groups, however. The National Rifle Association, veterans groups, hunters, and the general public in less-populated states where urban crime is not as much of a problem have been the most effective in opposing increased controls. Many resist further incursion by the government into what they consider their private affairs and particularly their "constitutional right to bear arms." Many of the opponents of such legislation also feel that there are sufficient laws on the books already, that the problem is one of enforcement, and that the imposition of additional restrictions would affect law-abiding citizens far more than those who are already using guns improperly.

The outcome has been few, if any, increased restrictions since the death of Robert Kennedy by means of a handgun in 1968 gave rise to much of the recent concern. A similar attack on President Reagan in 1981 gave little impetus to renewed efforts at controls and did not cause President Reagan to change his mind to become a supporter of such controls.

Is Mr. Ruger a model business executive, operating a very successful company in an ethical manner, or are he and his company to be criticized for not living up to their responsibilities? If you do wish to criticize him, what other manufacturers of legal products would you also criticize and why? How could you build a strong case, if you wished to, that such companies should take actions that will affect their profits as a result of turning them away from activities that are legal and approved of by their boards of directors?

ENVIRONMENTAL POLLUTION

A more widespread problem is the pollution of the environment, both in the manufacturing process and by the product in use. Companies have been much criticized in the last decade or so for not anticipating the problems and acting on their own rather than waiting for, and often opposing, legislation. In their defense, companies have pointed to the substantial costs that are involved in remedying many pollution problems and have argued that no company in a competitive economy can afford to spend much more money than its competitors, either on capital costs or operating costs, without suffering a disadvantage. And the costs are in fact substantial. It was estimated, for example, that the paper industry would have to devote about 21 percent of its total capital spending to meet pollution standards during the mid-70s and that the petroleum, iron and steel, and nonferrous metal industries would have to devote between 15 percent and 18 percent of their capital budgets to the same purpose.

Executives have also been quick to point out that because of the great increase in regulations and federal agencies, they have often had to plan under such uncertainty as to the applicable standards and available technologies that frequently the only prudent choice is to delay capital commitments for as long as possible. By the end of the 1970s, evidence was widespread that the substance of the regulations related to the protection of the environment as well as the approval process were also causing significant delays in new projects. Planning cycles were stretching beyond 10 years for major projects such as pipelines and power plants.

The uncertainties concerning nuclear plants were such that some experts were predicting that no more would be planned because of the lead times and uncertainties that existed. A major oil terminal and pipeline to the Southwest widely acknowledged as being essential to make efficient use of the oil arriving from Alaska had finally been abandoned by its sponsors in 1979 after many years of trying to receive the necessary permits from the many governmental units involved. At that point the administration, caught in the midst of the worst oil shortage since the 1973 Arab oil embargo, announced plans to create a new federal agency that would "cut through the red tape" for such essential energy projects as the pipeline.

Few would argue that our method of dealing with our environmental problems has been ideal, but there is little agreement on what better solutions might be. Many regard the laws and regulations as a necessary way to counter the "irresponsibility" of corporations. It is clear that practices which we do not now condone existed and would likely have continued to exist if laws had not been passed. It is also important to note that the standards of what is acceptable have changed considerably, partly because of the much greater knowledge that we now have about the harmful effects on the environment of a variety of industrial substances and wastes and partly because we have set higher health and aesthetic standards for our society in recent years. The regulations arose because individual companies did not, and individually perhaps could not, meet the expectations of society with regard to environmental protection. Were the regulations inevitable, or could more responsible leadership on the part of businesses or business executives have made a difference?

It is not necessary to provide detailed examples of each of the many types of issues that may arise under the umbrella of corporate responsibilities. There is much discussion of these issues in the press and much that is unique to the specific situation. The purpose of giving a few examples here is simply to point out the variety as well as the complexity of the problems in this broad area you will have to face as a general manager.

Public concern with the ethical level of business practice for its own sake, however, rather than with the results of that behavior, has increased greatly in recent years and warrants some further exploration. Two examples of corporate behavior that have received much attention in recent years are corporate investment abroad, particularly in South Africa, and "improper corporate payments," now covered by the Foreign Corrupt Practices Act of 1977. These will be discussed in turn.

CORPORATE INVESTMENT ABROAD

Because of the apartheid policies of the South African government, there has in recent years been a considerable amount of criticism of American companies with investments in South Africa. Strong external pressures have been brought to bear on companies to divest themselves of these holdings on the grounds that such investments help to perpetuate a morally corrupt regime. The nature of the investments is generally not an issue nor is the question of whether the employment practices of the American subsidiary are better than South African law or custom would dictate. Arguments that the employment and training made possible by that investment are important in the short run for South Africa's blacks, and that they may also contribute to the long-run improvement of the society, are not given much weight. Although the critics hope that the withdrawal would impose a hardship on the South African regime, the essential element of much of the criticism seems to be that the investment is simply morally wrong. To withdraw and to let someone else—South Africa or third-country interests—own and operate those facilities is seen as preferable to permitting American investments to remain within the country.

Some managers, as a result of conscience as well as pressure, spent a great deal of time dealing with this question. Managements have traditionally felt that their investment decisions in foreign countries should be determined largely by their own business judgment and the applicable national laws or guidelines. It has become apparent that significant and vocal segments of the public consider it a legitimate concern of theirs as well. One company which devoted significant top executive time to deal with this question, for example, was Polaroid, an innovative and highly successful company. And Polaroid found itself deeply involved in spite of the fact that it was commonly acknowledged that they would rank high on any list of "socially responsible" corporations, based on their operations in this country, and that their South African investments were minimal in terms of their overall business.

Other companies with more substantial investments in fixed assets or with a more important share of their revenues in South Africa were both more vulnerable to criticism and in a more difficult position in the event they did decide to withdraw. Even university and church investment committees became involved as a result of widespread attempts by various groups to persuade them to eliminate from their investment portfolios the securities of any companies doing business in South Africa.

Policies on investments in South Africa, as well as on the broader question of whether to invest in companies that came under criticism for the level of their corporate responsibility on any matter, were developed and widely debated. The most widely adopted set of principles with regard to South Africa was developed by the Reverend Leon Sullivan of Philadelphia. By early 1982 over 130 American companies, operating subsidiaries, or affiliates in South Africa had subscribed to principles calling for:

1. Nonsegregation of the races in all eating, comfort, and work facilities.
2. Equal and fair employment policies for all workers.
3. Equal pay for equal work.
4. Initiation of training programs to bring blacks into supervisory, administrative, clerical, and technical employment.
5. Recruitment and training of minorities for management and supervisory positions.

6. Improving the quality of life for minorities outside the work environment in areas such as housing, health, transportation, schooling, and recreation.

Over a hundred American companies doing business in South Africa refused to commit themselves to the Sullivan Principles, however. Their reasons included a disagreement with some of the principles, an objection to being pressured into subscribing to any set of principles at all, an unwillingness to meet the reporting requirements, or a reluctance to go beyond the laws or practices of the host country. As of 1984, the issue was far from resolved.

WATERGATE AND THE FOREIGN CORRUPT PRACTICES ACT

The enactment of the Foreign Corrupt Practices Act in December 1977 seems also to have stemmed in good part from a concern with the morality of the practices proscribed, and not just the direct consequences of the practices on American consumers or citizens.

In the course of the investigations of the Watergate scandal in the Nixon administration, it become evident that the Committee to Re-Elect the President (CREEP) had obtained substantial amounts of money from sources either illegal, unreported, or both. Further investigation uncovered a considerable number of corporate contributions for political purposes, clearly against existing laws. Critics alleged these were simply bribes offered by corporations to politicians in order to influence legislation and secure favors.

Corporations often said these contributions were demanded or expected of them as a condition for gaining business or for not losing business with federal and state governments. Numerous reports of repeated and insistent personal solicitation of corporate contributions by high administration officials were reported.

Extensive investigations and much highly critical publicity followed, and more than 300 corporations were eventually implicated. There were a number of stockholder suits to force the executives involved to repay to the corporation from their own resources the illegal contributions from corporate funds that they had made. Many of these lawsuits created a serious financial burden as well as personal trauma for the executives involved. Considerable personal legal costs were incurred by many individuals, and in addition there were a number of prosecutions and convictions of corporations and executives for having violated the law, although the penalties were generally modest fines of $5,000 or less.

Since hundreds of corporations were involved in thousands of individual cases of illegal contributions, there were presumably also many hundreds of individuals who allegedly received the contributions who could also be in violation of the same law. For example, the lobbyist for only one of the companies found guilty of extensive illegal contributions identified under oath that 117 U.S. senators or candidates for the Senate and about a score of contenders for governor had received illegal contributions from his company, surely one of the worst offenders. He added in his deposition that the U.S. representatives who had received illegal gifts were too numerous to identify with precision.

Leon Jaworski, special prosecutor during the period, was operating under a law which required the prosecution to establish that the recipient either knew that the political contribution came from a corporation or that he accepted such money in the "reckless disregard" of whether the source was a corporation or not. Mr. Jaworski stated that his ability to prosecute recipients had been severely limited by the the virtual impossibility of proving such knowledge, since the contributions were usually made in cash "from your friends at the X company." As a result, it appears that there were only two successful prosecutions of politicians for accepting illegal corporate contributions, and they were facilitated by guilty pleas.

The Senate itself seemed to show considerably less enthusiasm in assisting the efforts of the special prosecutor and others in investigating recipients of illegal contributions than in condemning those who made the contributions. In spite of evidence that the private law office of the then Senate minority leader had demanded and received semiannual payments of $5,000 from one of the companies for a number of years (the company's lobbyist testified under oath that a total of $100,000 had been paid), the Senate Ethics Committee refused to call witnesses in the matter, refused to open the senators' sealed financial records on file, and refused to turn over any information to the Internal Revenue Service. It also voted to drop its investigation of about two dozen other senators alleged to have received payments from the same company. Further complicating the efforts of prosecution by the Justice Department, Congress at about the same time shortened the statute of limitations for knowingly accepting corporate gifts or for failing to disclose gifts from the existing five years to three years, thereby placing a number of the alleged offenses beyond reach.

That the political contributions made by corporations were both illegal and improper is clear. That most of those who received the contributions escaped virtually unscathed, both in the eyes of the public as well as in penalties imposed by law, seems equally clear. Regrettable though the double standard of conduct and justice may seem, the important lesson to be drawn from the episode is not that business may have been treated unfairly. Instead, it is that you will not be able to excuse your own behavior by pointing to "common practice" or what others are doing. As a business executive you will need to conduct your affairs so as to avoid not only illegal practices, as these undeniably were, but also practices which may at a later date be viewed as morally wrong. That others may not be equally condemned will be of little comfort and no defense.

What led to the passage of the Foreign Corrupt Practices Act, however, was the further discovery that substantial amounts of money—in the millions of dollars for many companies—had been paid to foreign government officials over the years in efforts to secure business. In our usual sense of the word, many of these payments would be called bribes. They were justified by the companies which had paid them as being necessary to obtain the business because of the demands of the local government officials and the existence of foreign competitors ready to pay the bribes, as well as by the undisputed fact that the practice of bribing officals had been widespread for centuries in many of the countries involved. The payments were denounced by those concerned with the morality of the practice as well as by those concerned by the poor example this set for the rest of the world by the world's leading proponent of the free enterprise system.

A strict law establishing severe criminal penalties for individuals caught violating the law, as well as substantial fines for both individuals and companies, was the result. Included in the law was a section charging management with the responsibility for establishing internal controls to prevent violations of the law. Both management and the outside auditors became responsible under the law for seeing to it that the internal controls were satisfactory. It appears that management, the auditors, and the directors (and especially the audit committee of the board of directors) may incur individual liability if transgressions occur and the control systems are considered, on subsequent investigation, to have been insufficient. This liability can occur, it should be noted, totally apart from the direct involvement on the part of the manager, auditor, or director in the particular violation.

The supporters of this controversial law saw it as essential in improving the image of capitalism, and particularly American capitalism, in the rest of the world. They also pointed to the basic immorality of paying bribes to secure favors, totally apart from the issue of what others may think of the practice. In addition, they made the irrefutable argument that the citizens in a country in which officials in power have the opportunity to enrich themselves by means of bribes incorporated into the price of the products the government buys are hardly being well served by their rulers.

The critics of the bill, on the other hand, considered it unduly restrictive with regard to its definition of payments that are illegal, as well as an impractical and unjustified attempt to impose the American standard of morality on cultures where seeking and accepting bribes has been a practice for centuries. They pointed out that the practice would very likely continue regardless of what we desire or legislate. In addition, they pointed out that the products and services we were selling were generally available from countries such as England, France, Germany, and Japan, among others and that these countries had shown a remarkable lack of enthusiasm for developing international standards or for enforcing provisions such as ours on their own companies. As a result, it was argued, we would lose a significant amount of business at a time when we could ill afford it in terms of the serious balance of payments deficits the country was incurring, in large part because of the enormous increase in oil prices since 1973.

The principal reason for looking briefly at the history of the Foreign Corrupt Practices Act is not to enable you to debate the merits of the act but to point out how rapidly practices which the business community once thought were not a major concern of the broader society can become the subject of public scrutiny, disapproval, and legislation. Some companies managed to avoid most of the practices proscribed by the act long before its enactment on the grounds that for either moral or economic reasons (or both) they simply did not want to engage in the kind of business that required the payment of bribes, domestically or abroad. Companies that were not as strict in their standards before it became a legal requirement helped bring about the considerable public criticism of business that developed at this time and no doubt helped bring about a political climate that resulted in passage of the act.

In addition, many of these companies also found it necessary to spend considerable amounts of money and time conducting internal investigations and negotiating with the SEC concerning the amount of disclosure that would be required in public filings concerning their reliance on "questionable corporate payments abroad," as the practice was delicately called, to secure business. Several years before the passage of the act, the SEC held that such practices constituted a material fact for an investor with regard to his evaluation of the integrity of the management and therefore the merits of the company as an investment, and that such practices would have to be disclosed. This represented a substantial departure from the traditional standards for measuring materiality, which had been based on the size of the transaction in question in relation to the overall financial results of the company.

If the payments by the company had been entered as tax-deductible business expenses, however, disclosure of payments that would be considered bribes then created the possibility of prosecution for tax fraud by the Internal Revenue Service—a criminal violation—on the grounds that bribes are not deductible for tax purposes. This problem arose, it might be noted, even though foreign bribes— or domestic, for that matter—were not generally against the law at the time.

The act has been the subject of extensive debate since its passage in December 1977. It has been criticized on many counts, including its effects on the ability of U.S. companies to compete abroad and the failure of the SEC or the courts to clarify the provisions of the act. The Reagan administration launched a major effort to amend the act in 1981. The Government Accounting Office (GAO) recommended that business be provided with clearer guidance on the act's accounting provisions and that the criminal penalties in that part of the law be repealed. As of mid-1984, there was still extensive debate about the act, but no legislative action.

Just as with the question of the procedures by which our society has handled the problem of protection of the environment, you should explore the question of whether there is not a better way to improve certain business practices that most feel are distasteful, if not immoral, although perhaps a necessary evil. In a remarkably short time, the practices brought considerable discredit on business in general and caused expense and embarrassment for the individual managers involved.

COSTS

Actions taken in the name of corporate responsibilities to help the broader society often cost money and frequently require the time and talents of busy executives. Some of the things you may want to do, and perhaps you feel you should do, may be difficult to honestly justify in terms of the demonstrable economic interests of any *individual* company. Although an individual may benefit greatly from the contributions others have made to The American Cancer Society, the Salvation Army, the local YMCA, or private universities, it does not follow, regrettably, that it is in the best economic interest of any single individual to contribute. What charitable and educational contributions should a company make and why?

Problems such as the ones described above are likely to be incidental to the mainstream activities of the business and limited in their impact on the economic performance of the business. Other problems, such as basic investment decisions, may entail much greater economic consequences. How much responsibility does a company have to train workers and establish plants in depressed urban areas, as Control Data has frequently done, if it is riskier and more complicated than expanding in existing facilities or familiar surroundings? Do the automobile companies have an obligation to continue to invest in facilities and therefore employment in the depressed Michigan area if possible, or should the management place new investment in more favorable areas in the United States regardless of union and community pressure? Or should firms relocate overseas, thereby making U.S. unemployment and balance of payment deficits even greater but hopefully improving the competitive strength and economic performance of the corporation? Or would it be more "socially responsible" to remain in the industrial Midwest, continue with an industry wage structure 50 percent or more above most other industrial workers in the United States, and lobby for protective tariffs, quotas, or local content laws in order to stem the flow of imports?

The pollution problem caused by automobile exhaust emissions represents another issue of concern to society for which the solution does not come cost-free. The type of improvements required to meet legislated emission standards finally enacted required expenditures in the hundreds of millions of dollars for the necessary research and development work and manufacturing facilities. They also resulted in automobiles which were more expensive to buy, more expensive to operate, and had poorer performance than earlier models. The entire package was neither a financial nor a marketing department's dream, and it is easy to see why individual companies did not feel they could take the lead in reducing harmful exhaust emissions unless they were sure all others would follow.

It also seems apparent, however, that if anyone were in a position to anticipate the clearly unpleasant and harmful consequences of continued uncontrolled auto emissions in large urban areas such as Los Angeles and New York City, it should have been the larger automobile companies. If the companies had assumed more responsibility for calling attention to a problem that was bound to occur, perhaps they could have contributed to some form of industry solution earlier. Instead a solution was imposed much later via a stringent law, an adversary relationship with still another government agency developed, and the auto companies were criticized by many for being obstacles to the solution of a genuine problem.

Another example of the problem of incurring significant short-run costs for the individual company would be with regard to the safety characteristics of automobiles. Most safety features—such as collapsible steering columns, seat belts, air bags, safety glass, or improved crash protection—add more to the price of the car than most consumers would prefer to pay. In addition, many of these advances require considerable investment in tooling and machinery and are feasible only if built into all the models offered and not as individual options.

If a manufacturer chooses to add to the cost of his product by building in features that increase the cost above that of his competitors but the extra features are not perceived as being worth the extra cost by the customer, the manufacturer who chooses to be "socially responsible" is likely to suffer in the marketplace. Industrywide attempts to raise standards of safety and quality are sometimes effective, but because of the provisions of the antitrust laws, there is no practical way to enforce such provisions on competitors who do not wish to comply. Even concerted action on a voluntary basis may be judged to be in restraint of trade.

POLICING CORPORATE BEHAVIOR

A greatly complicating factor for business in comparison with professions such as law and medicine is that the broader business community has virtually no control over the behavior of the individual company and/or management that chooses to act in a grossly irresponsible manner, even though within the letter of the law. Indeed, it can be observed that unscrupulous practices on the part of one competitor not only go unpunished by the business community but sometimes result in pressure on others to reduce their standards as well. Furthermore, such practices on the part of a few can result in legislation affecting all.

The more established professions such as law and medicine have a clear advantage over business with regard to policing both the ethics and competence of their members. Standards for admission to the practice of the profession as well as standards of conduct for members have been developed by the professions themselves and are legally enforceable. That such internal policing methods have not solved all of the problems of either of those professions, however, is evident.

With regard to preventing distinctly harmful behavior on the part of those few who might follow that path in the pursuit of their own interests, it is often argued that the only effective course is government regulation. The passage of the Securities and Exchange Act in 1934 probably did more to eliminate certain abuses in the securities industry than 50 years of preaching by the more moral members of the community would have accomplished. Few of us, however, would like to see government regulation as the only means by which corporations can be influenced to use their broad powers responsibly.

SOCIETY AND CORPORATE RESPONSIBILTY

It is important to remember that private enterprise exists only by the consent of society and that the "rights" business has with regard to making decisions in its own interest can be abridged or modified by means of our democratic process. If enough people become convinced that a company should not be allowed to reduce employment in a given area without extensive consultation with local authorities, long notice, and the payment of very substantial termination costs, as is the case in many European countries, such laws will be enacted. If enough people become convinced that business would serve society's interests better under a plan of federal, rather than state, chartering of corporations, with perhaps labor and government representatives on the boards of directors of larger companies, that too will happen.

The difficult decisions for the manager are not with respect to behavior covered by law or regulation, even though they may have been matters that once were at the discretion of business. By far the more difficult questions involve those things a manager wants to do because they seem right—in a moral, personal, and ethical sense. The problem is to perceive what usefully can be done that is not required to be done to contribute to the broader goals of society and to undertake early and in good faith those things that society may later feel business was remiss in not undertaking. And while doing all of this, you will have to remember that your primary responsibility as a general manager is to maintain the economic health of the organization. Actions undertaken for reasons of corporate responsibility that severely affect the economic capacity of the enterprise to furnish employment and provide goods and services are not likely to be a net benefit to the society, let alone the shareholders.

Two trends seem evident. First, the public is coming to expect more of business enterprises than the traditional economic role they have fulfilled in the past. Even though business may not be the cause of many of the shortcomings of our society, their human and financial resources are increasingly being called on to help solve problems such as those of disadvantaged minorities, decaying cities, and pollution of the environment.

Second, it is clear that matters that once could be decided by managements based largely on their own personal values and sense of fairness have in many cases become regarded by the public as a responsibility of the corporation. These matters in turn have become the subject of law or regulation in instances where corporations were not meeting their responsibilities in the manner society thought appropriate.

LEGITIMACY OF POWER

In the preceding pages we have been concerned primarily with the proper exercise of corporate power, as seen by the broader public or significant segments of it. The power exists, and decisions must be made on how to use it. For those immediately affected by corporate decisions, the substance of those decisions is understandably the most pressing issue.

The legitimacy of that corporate power is a separate issue, more philosophical in nature, but important to some. No solution has as yet been found to the basic dilemma presented by Carl Kaysen that corporate power is illegitimate and therefore irresponsible because the people affected greatly by those decisions—employees, the community, and even the stockholders—very often have little or no real voice in the making of those decisions. The issue is not the substance of the decisions or the motives of management, but the right of management under our present system of corporate governance to make the decisions.[5]

There have been many attempts to influence both the substance of management decisions and the process by which they are made by the media, university and church groups, shareholders, and individual pressure groups. That several of these groups are, in Kaysen's sense, still irresponsible with regard to exercise of corporate power should be evident; the problem of legitimacy remains.

A more fundamental approach to the problem of corporate governance and therefore the legitimacy of the power that corporations have has been underway for some time by the Securities and Exchange Commission and others with regard to their attempts to change the composition of boards of directors to include more members "independent of management." Some plans include provision for the election or appointment of directors to represent special interests—such as the community, or the public or the employees—but these proposals have incurred considerable opposition on legal, philosophical, and practical grounds. The SEC has been aggressively expanding the responsibilities and personal liabilities of the directors for corporate misdeeds, however, and this trend will surely continue.

SUMMARY

The question of just how education can increase our awareness of the ethical issues and choices that you and others will face as managers, and hopefully provide you with a framework and a set of values which will result in behavior most people would regard as responsible, remains.

Based on our experience, simply reading about ethical choices in the abstract, divorced from specific situations, is unlikely to change behavior. Neither, unfortunately, is preaching. What a person considers ethical behavior is influenced strongly by the church, the schools, the family, and peers during childhood and early adolescence. If children have found that highly aggressive behavior, perhaps accompanied by minor chiseling or outright deception, has been a fruitful strategy, it is unlikely that the preachings of a professor will change their ideas of how to best achieve their goals. If such behavior continues to bring rewards, as it undeniably does in some cases, it is even less likely that the behavior will change. To analyze, discuss, and perhaps criticize the ethical behavior of others is much easier than bringing about a change in behavior.

We believe it will be most useful for you to put yourself in the position of the manager, with all of its competing demands and pressures and constraints, and to develop and defend your position before your peers. What degree of freedom do you have to do what you feel is right and desirable, and how can you create opportunities and new strategies or policies that will enable you to best meet all these competing demands? How can you be more farsighted than some managers have been and anticipate what needs to be and should be done before it becomes a crisis?

We have found it is most useful for you to state and defend your position to peers who may think you are doing either more or less than wisdom or morality would require. You might also consider whether you would be willing to explain to your family or on television your real reasons for your decisions. Values and sensitivity to ethical issues develop and change slowly, and they seem to us to be influenced more by the need to articulate and defend them to people important to you than by being told what they should be.

As a manager, you will not be able to avoid facing the basic question *"To whom am I responsible and for what?"* Your answer may be solely economic performance for the shareholders. If so, even though you operate within the requirements of the law, you will be doing less than most of us personally would like to do and less than could be expected of any healthy corporation. On the other hand, if you listen to and follow all who would put a claim on the company's resources and skills, the result is sure to be disastrous for the economic well-being of the company.

For the present, and even for the foreseeable future, there is no theory that will help you make decisions with regard to corporate responsibilities that would satisfy both those who cling to traditional legal and economic doctrines as well as those who view the corporation as an instrument of society available to help society achieve much more than the traditional economic goals. To help you achieve a proper balance in these matters is one of the goals of a professional education. A strategy which does not make any allowance for the pressures that exist and that will be brought to bear in the broad field of corporate responsibility, as it pertains to that particular company, industry, or community, runs the risk of being deficient by purely economic standards. More important, it may not take advantage of the opportunities private enterprise does have to make a contribution to the quality of life beyond what is required by current law, practice, or the threat of proposed legislation.

If management is to have any valid claim to being a profession, its members need to develop and maintain a set of personal standards and attitudes regarded as worthy by the broader society. Knowledge and skills and techniques directed at achieving economic goals—which are so much easier to teach and to learn—will not alone equip you to make the decisions in the area of corporate responsibilities that you will ultimately have to decide for yourself. To attempt to do good while also doing well, for both yourself and your shareholders, is a goal worth pursuing.

CHAPTER 8

An Approach to Strategy Implementation

In these next two chapters we ask you to shift your attention to the task the general manager faces in leading the organization in the accomplishment of the purposes identified and decided upon by the process described in the preceding chapters. Our concern will change from the formulation of strategy to the implementation of that strategy via the people in the organization. We will no longer be concerned primarily with determining the long-term objectives of the firm and developing plans to achieve them; but we will focus instead on the role of the general manager in designing the appropriate structure and processes and managing the overall organization. As in the preceding chapters on the process of strategy formulation, we will continue to deal primarily with single-business organizations.

The process of strategy formulation can be highly analytical in the usual sense of that word. It normally incorporates a large amount of information about the economic environment of the firm as well as data from the functional areas of the business such as marketing, production, and finance. Much of this data is in quantitative form, and formal models and analytical techniques are of great help in dealing with such data.

The administrative tasks and skills involved in designing the organization and leading its members in the accomplishment of its strategy are less subject to formal analysis and the application of quantitative techniques, however. Your problem now is the design and operation of structures and processes that will enable and inspire people to identify their own interests with those of the firm and thereby contribute to the implementation of the strategy of the firm.

The behavior of people in organizations will become your primary concern, and that will entail developing knowledge and skills in the so-called soft areas of business administration. What you have learned about human behavior from courses such as Psychology, Sociology, Organizational Behavior, and Management Accounting and Control is most likely to be of help to you in this task. Most valuable of all is likely to be the knowledge you have developed about people and the skills you have acquired in dealing with them through your own experience in organizations.

The concern of this chapter is one about which a great deal has been written. The challenge of motivating people in a free society to contribute their best efforts in the achievement of purposes for the most part established by others and for the benefit of others has been the subject of thought, research, and writing for thousands of years. Academic disciplines such as psychology and organizational behavior have arisen in part to deal with these problems. Specific courses dealing with the behavior of people in organizations and methods of measuring their performance exist in every school of business, and every business library is likely to have hundreds of books and thousands of articles which deal with these problems.

The preceding should lead any sensible reader to ask at this point what we can add to the knowledge you have already acquired in other courses and readings concerning the behavior of people in organizations. What you have learned elsewhere about interpersonal relationships, human motivation, measurement and control systems, organizational design, and leadership should surely be applicable to the general manager's task of leading the organization to the achievement of its strategy. We will be interested in the application of this knowledge, however, and not just in the knowledge itself. In that sense, your task in this part of the book will be broader than what you are likely to have been exposed to in other courses dealing with the topics described above.

PERSONAL SKILLS

As you develop your understanding of the problems of implementing a corporate strategy, you should make a special effort to also develop some of the interpersonal skills essential to the general manager. An understanding of the job and the intellectual ability to analyze problems, develop solutions, and recommend action to someone else is not sufficient. In dealing with organizations, the way in which you interact with people will play a large role in your effectiveness.

The most realistic setting for the development of such skills is, of course, on the job. The principal disadvantage of learning in such a setting is that the learning opportunities are quite unstructured and random in nature and that mistakes are costly. Fortunately the classroom process itself, especially when conducted by the case method, can provide a major learning opportunity in this regard.

Listening to others, learning to understand what they mean as well as why they are saying it, and convincing them of the merits of your position are important skills to learn. These skills will be even more essential to you in your job than they are in the classroom setting. Acting out, where appropriate, exactly what you would say or do in the specific situation is useful practice. Ample opportunities for such role playing exist in most case discussions.

A determined effort on your part at all times to be the person involved and to talk as though you were that person, not simply to advise him what to say, will emphasize the difference between recommending to another and acting yourself in the situation. You will find that it is very much easier to say what you think the president in a case you are discussing in class should tell an angry subordinate than it is to say it yourself to one of your classmates who is playing the role of the subordinate. To be able to see the situation from the viewpoint of another and to act as though you were in the situation yourself is the essence of the administrative point of view, and that distinguishes the effective practitioner from the scholar, observer, or critic.

APPROACH

To assist you in the task of implementing the strategy of the company, we shall suggest a simple framework, or approach, just as we did for the problem of strategy formulation. We will emphasize again that these two tasks of formulation and implementation are split apart largely in the minds and writings of students and observers; no manager can focus on one without considering the other. You will no doubt concentrate your attention on one aspect or the other as the occasion demands, but the overall achievement of purpose requires a blending of formulation and implementation suitable to the company. A brilliant strategy without a means of accomplishment is of no greater value than a superb organization without a purpose.

We suggest you think of the problem of managing the overall organization in terms of the sources of influence available to the manager in working with the organization. The tasks to be accomplished will be, in large part, the result of the objectives chosen and the strategies developed. The sources of influence that the manager has in leading the organization in the accomplishment of these tasks can be grouped into five categories:

1. The organization structure: the definition of responsibilities and the establishment of reporting relationships among individuals and subunits.
2. The information systems: the collection, flow, and presentation of information concerning the operations of the organization.
3. The reward systems: the multiple forms of rewards which can be earned by (or withheld from) the members of the organization, including pay, incentives of all kinds, praise and personal satisfaction, promotion, and so on.
4. The allocation of resources: the provision of sufficient monetary, physical, and human resources to units or projects, which not only is essential to the accomplishment of the objectives set out but also often becomes a source of personal satisfaction to the individuals involved.
5. The most intangible source of influence of all, but perhaps the most important, is what we commonly lump under the catchall of *leadership*: the overall behavior of the manager as it affects the desires and the abilities of the members of the organization to work toward the accomplishment of the organization's goals.

The totality of the general manager's job, then, can be thought of as developing and maintaining a strategy that is a creative and productive fit of the various elements that affect the formulation and the implementation of that strategy. Beginning with Chapter 2, we have been emphasizing the strategy formulation portion of this simple diagram; in this chapter, we will be adding the strategy implementation aspect. As explained before, the two are interrelated in practice, and each influences as well as is influenced by the strategy of the firm.

EXHIBIT 8–1
Formulation and Implementation of Strategy

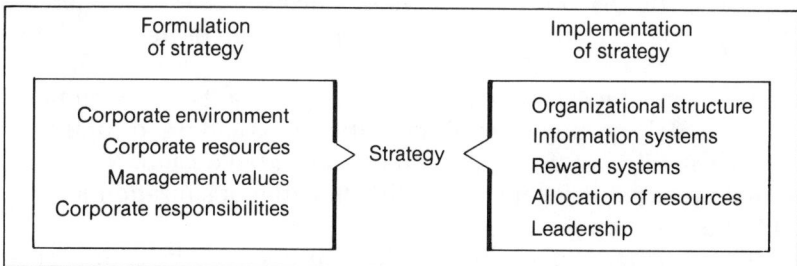

Formulation of strategy		Implementation of strategy
Corporate environment Corporate resources Management values Corporate responsibilities	Strategy	Organizational structure Information systems Reward systems Allocation of resources Leadership

Organization structure, information systems, reward systems, resource allocation procedures, and leadership are all familiar topics. With the exception of the nature of effective leadership, the sources of influence available are in themselves not overly complicated. Furthermore, there will be no lack of people ready to offer advice. Consultants in various aspects, such as organization structure, compensation schemes, or information systems, are always ready to assist you with the latest developments in their specialties. Your functional and staff subordinates will quite understandably each want to be in the forefront of good practice as well, and they are likely to offer their help also. Your challenge will be to develop the judgment required to combine the tools and advice available to all in such a manner that they are effective over a long period of time for your specific situation.

The test of effectiveness from the viewpoint of the general manager does not lie in the sophistication or even "correctness" of any one element but in the way that they fit together and reinforce each other to serve the broader purposes dictated by the strategy of the company. The best of everything is likely to be more than any company needs and more than most can afford.

We will proceed next to further discussion of the individual sources of influence you will have available to you in dealing with the implementation of corporate strategy, leaving the topic of leadership to the next chapter.

Organization Structure

Organization structures arose as a result of the need to divide the overall task to be done into parts that could be carried out by individuals but still coordinated to ensure effective results. This required a subdivision of tasks, a delegation of authority and responsibility, and a definition of reporting relationships. Organization charts are but maps designed to represent the territory.

The familiar black lines on the organization chart, however, along with titles and job descriptions that describe what the inhabitants of the boxes are supposed to do, imply a far neater and more rational world than exists in real life. Actual activities, if not formal job descriptions, will and should reflect to some degree the skills, interests, and power of the executives involved as well as the formally specified needs of the organization. No charts or descriptions can accurately portray all of these relationships and responsibilities, but that should not detract from the value of the organization chart as a starting point for understanding how the organization should and does function.

Even in most single-business organizations, where the functional vice presidents report directly to the president, many more relationships need to be taken into account in practice than those represented by connecting solid lines. The problem becomes much more pronounced in the multiproduct and multilevel organizations, discussed in more detail in later chapters. Where such alternate or dual reporting relationships are fairly clear, we tend to represent them by means of dotted lines. The term *dotted line relationship to* is often used, for example, with regard to division controllers who may have a solid line relationship to (be a direct subordinate of) the division general manager but who have a dotted line relationship to the group or corporate controller. Similar relationships can exist in the functional organization.

When the multiple relationships become so numerous that a chart showing all the appropriate dotted lines would resemble a drawing of a storm-battered spiderweb, we sometimes drop the lines altogether and describe it as a matrix organization, in which responsibilities for results are far more explicit than lines of authority. Such organizational forms are common in industries where large projects exist which require many months or years to complete, as in the defense industry.

The product manager form of organization, in which the person responsible for the success of a product line does not have much, if any, direct authority over the product development, manufacturing, or marketing functions that affect the success of his product line, can also be thought of as a matrix form of organization. In such organizations, results are expected to come less from reliance on formal lines of authority than on a common commitment to work together to do what needs to be done. Texas Instruments for decades has been a particularly dedicated and vocal proponent of this form of organization, which they refer to as "product-customer centered." Under this philosophy, each party is expected to resolve, in a constructive way, the conflicting demands often placed on them or on the resources under their control.

There is also a separate category of relationships brought about by the existence of staff personnel at various levels. The manager of facilities planning, for example, could be a subordinate of one of a number of executives, including the president. He is unlikely to have any direct authority over others reporting to those executives or to those who are below him in the organization except for those in his own department. His opinions and advice may have considerable impact on others in the organization who have no formal reporting relationship with him, however, and in a manner which is seldom spelled out explicitly. As with a number of other staff managers, such as those involved with personnel matters, capital budgeting, strategic planning, and the like, their influence often exceeds their formal authority. The appropriate role of staff and the ways in which staff personnel exert influence on people over whom they have no formal control is a never-ending source of debate between line and staff personnel.

Informal Organization

Beyond the complexities we try to represent by terms such as *line, staff, solid lines, dotted lines,* and *matrix organization* lies what we commonly call the *informal organization.* That is a euphemism for "the way things really work," and it covers everything about which we cannot be more explicit. It consists of the pattern of relationships and ways of working with each other that build up in conjunction with any formal organization structure and process or that arise even in the absence of such prescribed patterns of interaction. As described so well in the management classic by Barnard,[1] it is heavily influenced by the values of management concerning acceptable ways of behaving with regard to each other and in that way is similar to the current concept of organization culture.

To ignore formal reporting relationships and titles is, of course, a mistake; they constitute the starting point for both performance and analysis. Without some degree of formal structure and definition of tasks and reporting relationships, an organization, even if committed to a purpose, is little more than a crowd. To believe the formalities of the structure and processes can be so well specified that the informal workings of any organization can be ignored, however, is also a mistake. The comments of an experienced group vice president in a multibillion-dollar conglomerate are most instructive:

> Many of us, including the business schools, overemphasize the importance of organization structure. In a well-educated, successful society the human relations are the key. Relationships between people and trust in your fellow man are what count.[2]

As you deal with organizational problems in the classroom or in practice, your challenge will be to go beyond the formalities of the organization structure to discern how the organization actually does work in the particular situation with which you are concerned. Your objective should be to develop the ability to work with and influence the organization in all its complexities, seeming inertia, and apparent irrationalities. You will need to determine what key tasks need to be done particularly well in order to attain the corporate objectives, and then design the organization structure and all the supporting policies to facilitate the achievement of those tasks. Your goal is to elicit individual behavior that will help rather than hinder the achievement of the corporate objectives by directing attention where it is most needed. It is, after all, people that make the organization work, and not the other way around.

Information Systems

No manager can operate without effective information about the internal operations of the business and the relevant factors affecting the business in the external environment. The way in which managers obtain this information, however, varies widely.

In the smaller business, and especially one which the manager founded and is still running, the manager is likely to just "know" much of what is important. The knowledge comes from long familiarity with the operations and the market and can be remarkably effective as an aid to decision making even though it seems to be acquired and used in a disorganized way.

The more common situation, however, and the one which you are most likely to encounter, is the one where the manager must rely on the information systems within the company to provide him with the financial and operating data needed to monitor the progress and performance of the company and its position in the marketplace. Although a significant amount of the accounting information collected is required by the Securities and Exchange Commission or expected by investors and creditors, much of the same information is also useful to the manager.

A large amount of information that is purely internal, however, is necessary to the everyday running of a business. You will have become familiar with much of the accounting-based information in various courses dealing with management accounting and control. The information will have to provide timely data on money and material flows, which in less abstract terms means information about items such as inventories, receivables, and physical output. There is no point describing these in detail, as the design and operation of such information systems is a well-developed field of expertise. It will be your responsibility as a general manager to make sure that you *are* getting the proper information in a form usable to you, and interpreted for you where appropriate, and not just mountains of data which you and others will probably ignore until a crisis forces your attention to it.

You will also have to devise means appropriate to your business and your knowledge of it that will help you keep informed as well as possible of the great variety of nonaccounting information that you need to know to be an effective manager. This includes external information as diverse as what your competitors are doing, the important trends in your markets, and what your customers think about your products or services. Internally, it includes information about your people, what potential trouble areas may be arising, where weaknesses in the organization or its operations may be that are not yet reflected in the numbers, and so on. Much of this is difficult to obtain by means of a formal process. The effective manager is one who has developed the informal work and social contacts that enable him to be knowledgeable about a wide variety of matters that may affect the performance and health of the organization.

It is not just the general manager who has information needs, of course. The larger the organization, the smaller a proportion of the information essential to the running of the company can the general manager assimilate or act upon. In all but the smallest of companies, an important responsibility of the general manager with regard to the information systems is to make sure that the people within the organization have the information they need to do their jobs properly.

Decisions concerning what information should be available at what level are far more important than just the costs of alternative solutions. What information is available to whom has a major impact on the degree of decentralization within the company. The advent of the computer has been a double-edged sword in this regard. It has facilitated the provision of timely information where it is needed, but it has also made too easy the distribution of highly detailed information to levels much higher than seem appropriate.

Many approaches are possible to the development and use of information systems that will enable you as a general manager to obtain the information you need to lead the company in the implementation of its strategy. Harold Geneen of ITT fame was well known for his insistence on "facts, unshakable facts" before coming to conclusions about any business problem, and he devised an extremely elaborate system of controls to ensure that he and others had the facts available. His training as an accountant, his photographic memory for figures, his unending energy, and his preference for large and long meetings where any detail was fair game all contributed to a very strong numbers-oriented information system and method of control of a very large and diverse company.

Few managers are as systematic and rigorous as was Harold Geneen in obtaining the information necessary to manage the business. The more remote the corporate headquarters and the more diverse the product line, however, the more likely the information will of necessity consist of formal reports and quantified data. Perhaps the other end of the scale can be represented by the wise words of a long-time, successful hands-on operating manager, who said the best advice he could give to any general manager is "to wear out two pairs of shoes for every pair of britches." Regardless of the approach which suits you or the situation you are concerned with, proper information at all levels is the only way to avoid inaction or ill-considered action.

Reward Systems

Rewards, both monetary and nonmonetary, are of considerable importance to most people. Of the various sources of influence available to you as a manager, pay and promotion are among the most significant as well as the most studied and discussed.

The rewards one gains from employment are of course much broader and more complex than just the monetary benefits earned; and these other satisfactions may compensate for, or at least distract attention from, what are perceived as shortcomings in the financial arrangements. You will have been exposed to much in your Organizational Behavior courses concerning the many factors that make for satisfaction in a job environment, and we urge you to draw upon that knowledge. Self-esteem, pride in work well done, the opportunity for personal and professional development, and a climate in which individuals are treated with fairness and respect are important to most people.

Also of great importance are the signals you give to your subordinates concerning your opinions of them and their work. When you become engaged full time in your career, it will be useful to reflect upon how much time you spend thinking about what your superior thinks of you and why he made this suggestion or that comment concerning your work. Your subordinates will be just as concerned with your opinions of them, just as likely to read more meaning into your actions and comments than you intended them to convey, and just as certain to feel better after receiving justified praise and to feel worse when ignored or criticized.

Although financial rewards are but one of the ways in which the organization rewards its members for past performance and thereby provides incentives for future performance, for most people they are likely to be among the most important. Most people do, after all, depend on their jobs for their livelihood, no matter how much they might also enjoy their work and appreciate recognition for a job well done. The money itself may take on less importance over time because of the high levels of compensation being earned, diminished personal needs, or the effects of taxes. The level of compensation relative to one's peers is still likely to be important as a way of "keeping score" and measuring success in the job itself as well as standing relative to others in the organization. To think that all you will have to worry about as a manager is compensation with regard to rewarding your subordinates is naive, but to think that the level of compensation is not important to most people is equally naive.

In any large organization there is of course the need for some rationality and comparability in compensation plans, salary levels, and incentive awards. Managers often are caught in a dilemma. On the one hand, they would like to make the reward systems as objective and standardized as possible. In addition to being simpler, this avoids the unpleasantness of having to justify individual decisions to those who are performing poorly and minimizes the chances of criticism that personal feelings or biases enter into decisions. On the other hand, totally formula-based and objective measures frequently are unable to capture the full measure of the job done in view of differing conditions or changing circumstances. Managers often vacillate between the two extremes of primarily formula- and primarily discretion-based compensation systems, always hopeful that the shortcomings of the present system will not be replaced by the different shortcomings of the proposed system.

Much effort has been expended both by companies and by consulting firms to deal with these problems. Partly because of the different needs of various organizations and partly because of the many different preferences managers have with regard to how to deal with these problems, the variety of basic compensation schemes and incentive-pay packages that have been developed is large. It includes combinations of cash, deferred cash, stock, and a wide variety of fringe benefits. The term *cafeteria approach to compensation* has even come into common use to describe plans which enable employees to choose that combination which most suits their tastes.

There are a number of issues related to compensation and incentives that continue to plague practitioners. How much should you take into account either the personal aggressiveness or the personal needs of individual managers? How often should you match the offer a manager has secured from a prospective outside employer, even though you suspect he may have solicited it as a way of improving his internal bargaining power? To what extent should you base a manager's compensation on his contribution to the success of the company, as best you can measure it, and to what extent should it be based on his market value, or on his presumed willingness to leave (or not leave)? How much should you reward a manager for past contributions or excellent efforts, even if the current results are not up to expectations, perhaps for factors over which he has little control? We all like to be measured only on matters that we can control, but the general manager is often held responsible for results, not effort. At what level do we expect managers to share in the risks of the enterprise and not just be measured and rewarded for performance with regard to matters they can control?

Salary, bonus, and promotion are among the most powerful sources of influence available to you in rewarding the organization for past effort that has been worthwhile and for stimulating the organization to perform effectively in the future. Accurate information about the actual performance of people is essential to a rational evaluation, as is an understanding of the individuals and a sense of fairness for all concerned. There are many formulas available, but there is no one formula that applies to all.

Allocation of Resources

Another major source of influence you have as a general manager is your power to allocate resources to those projects, units, or people that you think need support in order to carry out activities important to the success of the business. Throwing money at problems may not solve the problems, but it is an unfortunate fact of life that most activities in a company require resources in order to be effective.

Although people and facilities are key in any significant activity of the company, money is the common resource that enables one to acquire the other resources needed. The systems within the company designed to deal with the allocation of funds for these purposes are the capital-budgeting systems and the budget review sessions where the focus is on ongoing or planned projects rather than the largely nondiscretionary spending required to maintain current operations.

There is an extensive literature and body of theory with regard to capital budgeting techniques that is derived from a theory of the firm as an economic unit. In this model, the sole objective is presumed to be the maximization of shareholder wealth, and the hurdle rates for capital requests can be derived from the firm's cost of capital and the presumed riskiness of the projects. All companies need some form of capital-budgeting techniques, and most are derived from this basic model.

In practice, things do not work quite so smoothly. As has been well documented by Bower[3] and others, capital projects are influenced greatly by the administrative context in which they originate and are evaluated. Many projects involve large elements of guesswork and judgment, and the more significant and innovative a project, the more uncertain these estimates are likely to be. In addition, many projects are not truly independent of all other projects or activities, and it is often most difficult to take these interdependencies into account. As a result, the financial returns that are projected are often the result of a considerable amount of judgment, optimism, provinciality, and even slight puffery at times.

As a manager with a vision of what the company wants to do and how it can get there, you have a responsibility to see to it that the resource allocation systems in the company support the require-

ments of the strategy. It is your job to see to it that sufficient resources are made available to those activities that are necessary for
the accomplishment of the broader corporate goals. Although simple
financial logic would lead one to argue that the strategy of the company is really nothing more than the sum of the most attractive
projects it can devise within the limits of the cash available and the
hurdle rates derived from the cost of capital, few managers are content to leave the future of the company to such a mechanical process.
Your judgment will be required in both the design and the application of the process in order to ensure that one of the essential influences you have over the direction of the company—the ability to
influence the allocation of people and money to various activities—
is being wisely applied.

PUTTING IT ALL TOGETHER

> We're not a marketing company, we're not an R&D company, and
> we're not a service company. We're a manufacturing company, and I
> believe that we are the best manufacturing company in the world.[4]

The above quote is from the president of the Lincoln Electric
Company of Cleveland, Ohio, whose strategy and unusual approach
to organization and motivation has resulted in a high level of productivity and economic performance over a long period of time.
Lincoln is an interesting example (more fully described in the case
referenced above) of a company which has succeeded in putting it
all together in a way that has served their purposes well.

Lincoln has achieved a leading position worldwide as a supplier
of electric arc-welding equipment and supplies, a mature industry
by most standards and one in which patents are relatively unimportant. Lincoln's strategy for many decades has been to concentrate on
a well-defined product line and to concentrate on building quality
products at a lower price than its competitors. That it has been able
to achieve this with overall compensation levels twice those of most
of its competitors implies a remarkable level of productivity. Its success has been based on the combination of a simple but durable
product strategy and a clear approach to the organization and motivation of the members of its organization, which it refuses to categorize as "workers" and "management."

Lincoln is perhaps best known for its highly unusual compensation policies, which have for decades provided a yearly bonus for
all its employees about equal to what is already a competitive base
salary. Since the company is strongly committed to individual rewards based on individual performance, in most years some factory

employees have earned three times as much as their counterparts in other companies.

There are a number of other practices and policies, however, which the management credits with establishing an overall atmosphere that enables the company to consistently reduce its costs, improve its market position, and earn profits sufficient to fund its own growth without recourse to outside equity or debt financing. These include a policy of hiring in only at entry-level jobs and promotion only from within, guaranteed employment after two years, frequent discussion of all factors affecting the work environment and productivity, attempts to minimize rather than emphasize the distinctions between various levels of employees, a very flat organization structure with little staff and no "assistants to," and highly predictable employee relations policies, frequently discussed and consistently enforced. That the combination of policies has been attractive to their employees is attested to by their remarkably low turnover rate—about one eighth that of comparable companies.

The point is not whether the specific practices of Lincoln, many of which are described above, can be transferred as a package to any other company, although much of what they do is worth serious consideration by all companies. More important is an appreciation of the success it has been able to achieve to date by the intelligent combination of a relatively simple but durable strategy combined with an approach to the implementation of that strategy that is effective for the company in its situation. Putting it all together effectively, not the creation of individually brilliant pieces, should be your objective.

SUMMARY

We have thus far described an approach to the task of implementing a strategy for a company which emphasizes the use of five basic sources of influence that are available to you as a general manager: the organization structure, the information systems, the reward systems, the allocation of resources, and your own leadership abilities. The emphasis throughout has been on the effective combination of these elements, not the development of any one element considered in isolation of the others and the strategy of the company. We will discuss leadership, the last of the sources of influence described, in the next chapter.

There are three factors that you should keep in mind as you attempt to use the various sources of influence described in a consistent way to effectively deal with the problems you encounter in cases or on the job.

First, you will be dealing with specific companies with specific problems, administrative histories, and strategies which define purposes, key tasks, and constraints. It is highly desirable to attempt to generalize about how categories of problems similar to those you are faced with should be solved, but those generalizations must be applied to the problem at hand. Your task is to give specific recommendations to the manager involved, not just demonstrate your knowledge about the characteristics of the ideal management-control system, compensation system, or organization structure for geographically decentralized firms.

Second, in dealing with the specific case situation, you will have to keep in mind that you are also dealing with real people, not idealized or typical people. You will frequently not know as much about the individuals as you would like, but at least do not ignore what information is available. You would not need to know much about Edwin Land of the Polaroid Corporation, the founder and inventor who has spent a lifetime developing the field of instant photography, to surmise that recommendations to enter the conventional photographic markets would not likely be well received. You will have to take into account the values of the people you are dealing with if you are to make either your actions or your advice useful.

Last but most important, your task will be the design of organization structure and processes and the management of its members as a means of achieving the overall purposes of the organization, not just the goals of the individual units or specialties. And though we all desire a humane and satisfying work environment, that environment must also be effective in meeting organizational as well as individual goals. Organizations in which individual efforts do not contribute sufficiently to the attainment of organizational goals seldom prosper and sometimes fail, at least in the private sector. If an organization depends upon the voluntary support of its customers, the feedback from the marketplace will inevitably determine the success or failure of the enterprise and the rewards that accrue to its members and owners.

CHAPTER 9

The Manager as Leader

Throughout history the personal skills and characteristics of the leader have had a major impact on the willingness of people to commit themselves to the leader's goals. The study of leadership and the attempt to generalize about the nature of effective leadership in organizations has long fascinated observers. Leadership in the church, in government, and in business has been studied from many different viewpoints by people from a variety of disciplines and backgrounds, and the literature relating to leadership is large.

The challenge we wish to present you with in this chapter is to develop a viewpoint and an understanding of leadership that will be useful to you in developing your own skills at performing that function as a leader of a business organization. Not everyone is suited to become, or wants to become, a leader. No manager can be an effective manager, however, without recognizing and meeting the needs for leadership of the organization for which he is responsible.

Our fascination with leadership comes from the recognition that leaders can have an enormous impact on the institutions they represent or command. The character and skill of the leader is recognized as a major factor in the behavior and performance of the institution or organization which he leads. As members of our society, we all have a legitimate interest in how well our major institutions, governmental as well as business, function. At a more personal level, we recognize the importance leaders play in matters that affect us in our daily lives more directly. How well the organization we work for is able to provide us with income, security, and a decent and, hopefully, challenging work environment is important to all of us.

LEADERSHIP STYLES

Many ways of classifying and describing styles of leadership exist. Perhaps one of the simplest and most familiar is the "Theory X–Theory Y" classification of Douglas McGregor.[1] In greatly simplified terms, the Theory X-type manager, described as being more commonplace in industry, manages on the assumption that his subordinates require a great deal of direction and follow-up, take little pride in what they are doing, and will only work hard if forced to do so. The Theory Y manager, rarer but by implication the more humane and effective leader, works on the assumption that subordinates can be highly motivated to perform their tasks with a minimum of supervision and direction, and that the principal task of the leader is to facilitate the release of these energies.

A broader description of various leadership styles can be found in a classic article by Tannenbaum and Schmidt entitled "How to Choose a Leadership Pattern."[2] They describe the range of possible leadership behavior available to a manager in terms of a continuum, as shown in Exhibit 9–1.

EXHIBIT 9–1
Continuum of Leadership Behavior

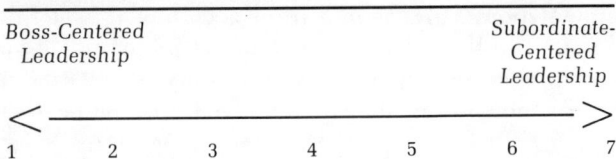

Boss-Centered Leadership	Subordinate-Centered Leadership

$$\longleftarrow \text{—————————————————} \longrightarrow$$

| 1 | 2 | 3 | 4 | 5 | 6 | 7 |

The numbers on the scale represent a series of arbitrary points along a spectrum of authority, with the most retention of authority by the manager represented at the left and the most delegation of authority to subordinates represented at the right. The various points are described as follows:

1. Manager makes decision and announces it.
2. Manager "sells" decision.
3. Manager presents ideas and invites questions.
4. Manager presents tentative decision subject to change.
5. Manager presents problem, gets suggestions, makes decisions.
6. Manager defines limits; asks group to make decision.
7. Manager permits subordinates to function within limits defined by superior.

The authors argue that the types of leadership that are practical and desirable depend in large part on three main factors: the manager himself, his subordinates, and the nature of the situation. They further argue that "the successful leader is one who is keenly aware of those forces which are most relevant to his behavior at any given time" and "is able to behave appropriately in the light of these perceptions."[3]

A slightly different way to think about the role of the leader in any specific situation is to consider the extent to which the leader is concerned about the *process* by which decisions are made as opposed to the *substance* of those decisions. In the one case you would become much involved in the details of a pricing decision, or a purchase of a new machine tool, or a personnel decision; in the other case, you would concentrate on developing and monitoring the procedures by which such decisions are made. The more you are involved in the substance of decisions that are within the responsibility of your subordinates, the more they will feel authority has not been delegated.

Your involvement in the substance of decisions is likely to increase in proportion to the importance of the decision and the expertise and interest you have in the matter under consideration. Management consists of developing procedures by which others can make the decisions one man can no longer make alone, however. The balance arrived at will be influenced not only by the personal style and preferences of the manager, but also by the time available to deal with the substance of decisions. The nature of the decisions in which the president can become substantively involved differs greatly in the multi-business company as compared with the single-business company, as we will explore in later chapters.

Zaleznick, approaching the topic in a very different way, argues in a stimulating article that the key distinction is between *managers* and *leaders* as he carefully defines those terms.[4] He states that managers are needed to maintain the balance of operations, but leaders are needed to create new approaches and imagine new areas to explore. He adds that since these are basically different types of people, it is difficult for one person to be both a manager and a leader, and the organizational environment that develops and rewards managers may stifle the development of leaders. "It takes neither genius nor heroism to be a manager," he notes, "but rather persistence, tough-mindedness, hard work, intelligence, analytical ability, and, perhaps most important, tolerance and good will." He argues that our society badly needs leaders in both public and private institutions but that we have become much better at training managers than leaders.

You have no doubt been exposed to many other points of view in addition to the few examples described above concerning styles of leadership and the characteristics or traits that contribute to successful leadership. With regard to Zaleznik's argument, one can argue that the person who is responsible for an organization will have to do the best he can as both a manager and a leader as the occasion demands, even though ideally such roles might require different people. As the title of this chapter indicates, that is a premise underlying the approach to the job of the general manager that we have been developing.

The processes of strategy formulation and implementation can be separated for intellectual reasons, as we have done in this book. They are interrelated in practice, however, and both are the responsibility of the general manager. So it is with the skills and behavior Zaleznick has categorized as characteristic of a leader or a manager. They are different and useful to separate for purposes of analysis, but as a general manager you will in most cases have to fulfill both roles as best you can. Effective leadership depends on a successful matching of the needs of the situation with the skills and personality of the leader. We are all limited in the extent to which we can modify our behavior or acquire new skills. Success as a leader is more likely to come from a steady development of skills and the attempt to match those skills to the requirements of the job than from a blind pursuit of a style that happens to have been successful for others with different skills in different situations.

Consider, for example, the following extremes of leadership behavior and skills. The Reverend Sun Myung Moon, founder of the Reunification Church (whose adherents are better known as "Moonies") is a charismatic and very effective leader of an organization which is, in addition to its religious nature, a substantial business undertaking and financial success. Robert McNamara, by all accounts brilliant and highly analytical, was an excellent business executive who became one of the most influential secretaries of defense America has had. Both have been the subject of strong criticism from some for either their objectives or policies or both. Few would argue, however, that either could have been equally effective in the other's organization.

We all know it is common to seek different types of executives for different strategic challenges—some managers are thought suitable for growth situations, others for mature businesses, and so on. So it is with regard to the need for a match between your own abilities and the demands of your job. We are all subject to the demands of our own environments and the limitations of our own skills and abilities. Each can be influenced or developed to some degree as you seek the combination which results in personal and organizational effectiveness; but choosing a leadership style is not quite as easy as picking a product off a shelf in a store or sitting down and learning a new analytical technique. Leadership skills develop and change slowly and stem from basic traits and abilities over which you have limited control. Your objective should be to improve your own leadership skills over time and to choose the situations in which you apply them so that demands of your job do not for long exceed your ability to perform effectively.

The challenge is to use your leadership skills to design the organization structure and tailor the information systems, reward systems, and the pattern of resource allocation to serve the strategy of the company. These areas of influence open to you must be designed and administered in such a way that the members of the organization both want to and are able to work effectively under your leadership in the furtherance of corporate goals. In meeting this challenge, several broad areas are worth your continuing attention.

REWARDS AND BEHAVIOR

It is unfortunate that the establishment of high rewards for narrowly defined performance can lead to behavior clearly not in the best interests of the corporation. The temptation to emphasize short-run profits at the expense of long-run development is but one familiar manifestation of this. Every once in a while there are articles in the press on more serious aberrant behavior that can result from high pressure for performance.

In a recent example, division personnel in a major corporation falsified records over a period of years to show increased profits of $8.5 million, which was sufficient to result in the involvement of the SEC, delay of the annual meeting, and much publicity and consequent embarrassment to the company. "When we didn't meet our growth targets, the top brass really came down on us," one former executive stated. "Everybody knew that if you missed the targets enough, you were out on your ear."

Similar pressures have led, for example, to instances of falsification of automobile exhaust emission tests, violation of pollution laws, and illegal payments of bribes in violation of corporate policy and (later) the law in efforts to secure business, all without the knowledge of higher levels of management. Many observers have attributed much of the reason for the extensive price-fixing that took place in the electrical equipment industry in the 1960s, as well as many later violations in other industries, to the desire on the part of managers to earn bonuses or promotions by performing well on the measures established or, in some cases, to avoid demotions or even loss of jobs.

As the rewards and punishments associated with performance increase, the temptation to do what is not in the best interests of the company or what is ethically or legally wrong increases. The challenge for you as a manager is to find that productive middle ground in which people will be motivated to expend their best efforts, but not in such a manner as to bring trouble to their companies or themselves.

COOPERATION AND COMPETITION

The responsible, effective general manager will want to keep track of the cooperative-competitive dimension of the working relationships within the organization. It is unavoidable that some will progress faster and further than others in all organizations; the traditional pyramidal form of organization ensures that. Since the positions higher in the organizational pyramid generally involve more money, prestige, power, and (hopefully) personal satisfaction, the matter of who is chosen for promotion is seldom a matter of indifference to the contenders. Even if promotion is not a factor, current pay and incentives are often structured to provide the maximum rewards to those performing the best on the measures used. That is the purpose of reward systems: to provide an incentive to continued good performance in the future by rewarding good performance in the present.

As in any field of competitive endeavor, however, it is necessary to establish limits as to what kind of behavior or degree of competition is acceptable. The question of what constitutes "acceptable competitive behavior" has surely arisen for each of you with regard to the various organizations and groups of which you have been a member. Parents learn to establish and enforce standards of behavior within the family; referees and umpires enforce the rules in sports; the manager, who unavoidably has such a strong influence on the "rules of the game," must do likewise. If you do not, you will soon find that rewards for individual performance can combine with personal ambitions to create an atmosphere which discourages cooperation and is less than satisfying to many who have useful contributions to make to the organization.

As an example of the power of simple techniques to affect both the competitive relationships and the working environment within an organization, consider the approach which was followed for a period of time by a major consulting firm in scheduling the workloads of their staff, deciding what new engagements they could accept, and planning their hiring requirements.

It was the practice to appoint project leaders for each of the engagements for clients, and these project leaders would then plan the amount and type of work that would have to be done and assemble the people they would need to finish the job on time and under budget. The assignment of consultants to jobs was therefore, in effect, done by the various project leaders, who had to decide which consultants to employ, taking into account the rates they would be charged for different consultants as well as when and for how long the consultants would be available to work on that project. The work schedule for individual consultants would then consist of their backlog of commitments to various project leaders, with unallocated time charged to "personal development" or "new business development."

The project leaders did not bargain with the consultants available on the basis of rates; these were determined periodically by the company. The internal rate charged for each consultant was influenced by demand, however, as were the pay and promotion prospects. It was, in effect, an internal market system under which project leaders bid against one another for the use of resources already under the control of the firm.

As a means of helping the project leaders in their scheduling task as well as collecting information useful in coordinating the new commitments of the firm with the available resources and the planned hiring schedule, charts were kept showing the workload by consultant and by project. At one point it was decided to post these charts for all to see and to update them once a week. Who was in demand and who was not therefore became public knowledge within the firm. The weekly posting understandably became an item of considerable interest to all and of embarrassment to some. What do you suppose the effects of this simple decision to post this information were? Did it encourage cooperation, or did it not matter in this case? Did it encourage greater effort by all? How would you like to work under such a visible control mechanism? What would be the likely overall effect on the attitude, behavior, and composition of the professional staff? It is questions such as these to which you will want to apply your judgment—not just to the technical aspects of evaluation or reward systems.

We face the paradox that we want the organization to be highly competitive in its external relationships with other organizations, but we wish to limit the internal competition so that it does not affect the incentives for individuals to work cooperatively as they do battle with the external world. We want the marketing department to regard the competitor's sales force as the enemy and to aggressively expand sales, much as we expect a boxer to consider his opponent as the enemy to be beaten. We do not, however, want this attitude to affect the ability of the marketing people to develop a team spirit and to work cooperatively with each other when that is to the advantage of the company, even though we may offer individual sales commissions. Neither do we want our own manufacturing and marketing departments to overlook the corporate interest as one fights to keep manufacturing costs and inventories down while the other wants a variety of products available in the field on short notice.

It is essential to do the best job possible in attempting to measure and reward individual performance within the organization. Unfortunately, individual performance can sometimes be achieved at the cost of—or at least without regard for—the performance of others and the overall objectives of the company. Balancing the cooperative-competitive dimension is a difficult judgmental task and one which requires continuing attention.

There has been much attention of late to the very different emphasis in Japanese management practice with regard to individual versus group incentives. Japanese managers are explicit about their belief in the importance of fostering group and company loyalties and are generally opposed to reward systems that are based on individual performance to the extent commonly found in this country.

There is much about the Japanese culture that emphasizes group membership and contribution over individual performance, however, and managerial approaches are not independent of the cultures in which they exist. The Japanese have been most effective with a system in which the "nail that sticks up is pounded down," but American practice is still predicated on a strong belief in the greater value to the organization of encouraging, measuring, and rewarding individual contributions.

The tools and techniques by which you can increase or reduce the amount of internal competition and affect the broader working environment are well known. Significant rewards based on clear measures are certain to influence behavior toward the attainment of those rewards; that is their intent. The shorter the time period of measurement and the greater the rewards, the more the behavior will be directed to the attainment of the rewards to the exclusion of everything else. If a broader concern for the overall performance of the company or cooperative behavior is unrewarded—or even worse, a handicap in the individual performance race—there is little reason to be surprised if not much of either occurs.

Rewards based on performance and the competition that follows for advancement in pay and position contribute in a major way to effective overall performance in most organizations. The challenge is to employ the tools and techniques affecting internal cooperation and competition wisely and responsibly.

AUTHORITY AND RESPONSIBILITY

If one person could actually perform all of the tasks necessary in the conduct of a business, the problems of management would be simplified considerably. The sole proprietor need not be concerned with organization charts, job descriptions, formalized compensation systems, or delegation of authority. If you are the only follower, it is not hard to be a leader. Most of the things we talk about in this chapter would have little relevance to the manager who works for himself.

As the demands of the business require the addition of people, however, problems of splitting up what needs to be done unavoidably arise. Our largest companies have hundreds of profit centers and thousands of people classified as managers, each responsible for the actions of units reporting to them. When the managerial tasks have been subdivided, problems of coordination inevitably follow. Information on what various units are doing is necessary not only to ensure that the efforts are complementary but to monitor progress, help in planning for the future, and evaluate the performance of the people involved so that they can be properly rewarded for their efforts.

It would of course be ideal if the overall needs of the company could be subdivided into tasks that were perfectly clear, with sufficient authority given to each subordinate manager so that he could control all of the key factors affecting the performance for which he will be held responsible. Under these conditions we could then evaluate and reward him on the basis of clear objectives related to performance over which he would have considerable control. Authority would be commensurate with responsibility, rewards would be based on explicit and controllable performance measures, the principles of management would have been complied with, and all would live happily ever after.

The preceding is a better description of the goals of an organization structure, information system, and reward system than it is the result of such systems in practice. Because of the unavoidable complexities of most management jobs, such ideal conditions are seldom attained. If you have set such goals for yourself as a general manager, be prepared to accept something less than perfection for a while. And if you expect to encounter such ideal conditions as you are working your way up in the organization, be prepared for some disappointments.

A more realistic set of observations about the relationships between authority, responsibility, and evaluation that exist in most organizations and that you are likely to encounter as you progress up through the management ranks are the following:

1. Your responsibilities are likely to exceed your authority for a long time. You will be expected to work with the people and the organization to secure by means of persuasion and logic the cooperation and resources you cannot command.

2. The evaluation of your performance will seldom be completely explicit. Judgments and opinions not clarified either before or after the evaluation period will be important. Furthermore, the basis of evaluation is likely to become less clear and explicit the higher up in management you progress.

3. Your superiors will always talk about the importance of not sacrificing the long-range in order to achieve the short-range goals. If your time perspective is longer than that of your superiors, however, you are likely to find yourself in trouble for failing to meet short-run goals important to them. You have the difficult job of achieving an acceptable balance between these conflicting objectives.

4. Decisions concerning evaluation and reward systems may often be influenced more by what will improve performance than by matters of fairness or logic. Giving a person conflicting objectives or holding him responsible for more than he can control may be neither fair nor logical, but it is used at times in most organizations because it is sometimes unavoidable and often effective.

5. Your boss probably knows better than you do the conflicts, illogicalities, and possible unfairness of the system under which you have to work. Probably he is now operating under more pressures and conflicts than you are. He learned to perform well in your environment, probably by not becoming overly disturbed by the matters discussed above but by concentrating instead on doing what needed to be done, trusting that in the responsible and effective organization competent effort would be recognized and rewarded regardless of the formalities of the system.

As you move on to jobs of increasing responsibility, you may be able to use your increased power, wisdom, and experience to change some of the inconsistent or frustrating factors you experienced when you were in those positions. If so, your subordinates will surely thank you for it. On the other hand, you may also come to the conclusion that such conflicts and frustrations are not necessarily undesirable from the viewpoint of the organization as a whole, that they can in a few cases be resolved completely anyway, and that your most constructive role is to strive for a balance between rationality and practicality.

It might be useful to ask yourself periodically just what you think your boss really expects of you and not just what the formalities of the measurement system are. Most likely he is just as smart as you are, has more experience than you do in the organization, and probably understands your position and pressures better than you give him credit for. He knows as well as you do that there are actions you could take to look good in the formal measurement systems that would be unwise from a broader perspective, and he has some of the same pressures himself. It is easy to lose sight of the fact that good performance on your part very likely helps him with his problems; it is easy to forget how much you have in common.

FAIRNESS, RESPECT, AND PARTICIPATION

Treating people with fairness and respect and, whenever possible, affording them some participation in matters that affect them are good business and good ethics. Strong unions arose in this country in part because management used its power poorly with respect to these matters. Hiring and promotion policies could be arbitrary, capricious, and based on favoritism, and there was little that workers could do about it other than form a union for the purpose of establishing a collective defense.

The emergence of strong unions has brought many problems to management, workers, and the competitiveness of the overall economy, but it has also resulted in a large number of rules which have limited many of the abuses of 50 years ago. To use just one example, the power to dismiss at any time for any reason was commonly used as a weapon by management in eliciting effort and obedience; both union rules and the practices of enlightened managements provide for much more of a due process in such matters now. It is, ironically, only the management ranks that are largely subject to dismissal at any time, although recent court decisions are moving slowly in the direction of a presumption of a right to continue in a job in the absence of clear evidence and warnings of unsatisfactory performance.

The issue of corporate governance and the representation of workers on boards of directors, as is now mandated by law for most of the larger German companies, is in part a broader manifestation of the drive for participation or at least input to decisions and the desire to be treated fairly and with respect. As a manager, you will have to channel these uniform human desires in ways that are economically sound and morally proper.

TRADING PLACES

In most of this book we have looked at the job of the general manager from the top down rather than from the bottom up. James F. Lincoln, in one of his "Observations on Management,"[5] observed that "If a manager received the same treatment in matters of income, security, advancement, and dignity as the hourly worker, he would soon understand the real problems of management." You will understand your task of managing the organization better if you form the habit of always putting yourself in the place of a subordinate as well.

How would you respond as a subordinate to the new goals or changes in the incentive plan or reorganization you are considering for the organization? How long before you would see through changes that are presented in a less-than-honest fashion? Even if the changes and reasons for them are well understood, how would they affect your motivation and morale if they were not in your interests? You do not need to feel that you are pandering to the needs of your subordinates in order to give some thought to how their jobs, careers, and attitudes about work could be affected by changes stemming from the organization's needs. If you find yourself perplexed at times by why your subordinates behave as they do, you should give more thought to how you yourself would act if you were in their place.

SUMMARY

The accomplishment of purpose is achieved by means of people working together on a voluntary basis. As a manager you will have considerable opportunity to influence or guide that behavior, but only in rare instances can you completely direct it on a continuing basis. The challenge is to devise structures, procedures, rewards, and an overall working environment that make possible the enthusiastic support for what needs to be done and not just the compliance with what the boss dictates or what the policy manual says. The former describes an organization made up of individuals for whom the achievement of personal goals contributes significantly to the overall goals of the organization. If you can relate the needs of your people to the needs of the organization in this manner, success cannot be far behind.

As the leader of the organization you will have to accept responsibility for problems that existed before you arrived and for conditions over which you have little control. Parties external to the corporation will bring their irreconcilable complaints to you, and your own employees will consider you to be more responsible for what happens within the corporation than is likely warranted. You will have to get the job done through others who, like you, are neither perfect nor devoid of other goals, interests, and responsibilities.

As you rise through the managerial ranks, your technical abilities and skills are likely to become relatively less important to you in the performance of your job. More important will be the ability to recognize and deal with issues beyond your own experience and specialized training. You will need to develop the ability to conceptualize and communicate the problems in such a way that others can understand and be convinced of their importance. Progress will come from organizing and motivating those with specialized knowledge and skills to apply their efforts to the constructive solution of the problems. In addition to conceptual skills, effective leadership requires the ability to break down problems into manageable parts for which tasks can be assigned and progress measured. You will need to be good at gaining support and commitment for what you think needs to be done, in spite of the different interests and positions of those on whose help you rely.

Research designed to discover the traits of successful managers has generally not resulted in strong conclusions, and we have not explored that avenue greatly. Instead, let us suggest a number of elements in the management of organizations that can be strongly influenced by the general manager and that contribute to the health and success of the organization:

1. Clear rules, fairly and consistently enforced.
2. An interest in and respect for the work done at all levels in the organization.
3. Respect for all as individuals and a minimum of distinctions based on level.
4. Leadership by example, especially in matters of integrity, effort, and loyalty.
5. Rewards related to performance and consistent with the goals of the enterprise.

Idealistic as some of these may sound, they do not imply an organization that is "soft." Listening to employees and treating them with dignity does not imply abdication of authority or lack of high performance standards; and enforcing rules will mean that those who are unwilling to abide by them or unable to contribute sufficiently to the goals of the corporation may have to leave.

None of the above is likely to be effective, however, unless the approach to implementation is designed to fit the strategy of the company. Policy formulation and implementation are intertwined, and the test of each can only be in the results of the combination. Organizational policies suitable for a rapidly growing, high-technology company are not likely to be the same as those for a low-cost competitor in a mature industry, even though the major elements suggested above apply equally well to both.

The requirements of the strategy determine what the key tasks are that the organization needs to do well for competitive success. It is your job as leader to see to it that these, above all, are done well. If they are not, it will not help much that the less important tasks are perfectly performed.

There is one thing you can conclude with confidence about the issue of leadership. If the answers to questions concerning the nature of effective leadership were simple, the literature on leadership would not be so voluminous. You can best develop your skills by testing what you know about leadership for its usefulness in helping you achieve a match between your own abilities and the requirements of the specific situation you face as general manager. You have but limited control over each, but each can be modified over time.

The breadth and challenge of the task of general management was well expressed by Dr. Edwin Land, founder of Polaroid, shortly before his retirement as chairman:

> There are men who organize ideas and men who organize people. It is the duty of the latter to protect the power of the former. While exquisite precaution is required in the control of the massive sums spent in the final stages of manufacturing, distributing, and advertising, as well as talent and inspiration, these later stages of corporate life are completely dependent on the profundity and validity of the initiating ideas. The significance of the initiator must not be hidden by the grandeur of the concluders.[6]

PART 3

The Multi-Business Company

CHAPTER 10

The Diversified Firm: An Overview

In this final part of the book we turn to the general management problems of the diversified firm. The preceding text has been primarily concerned with the task of the general manager in either single-business firms or subunits of diversified firms—which are similar to single-business firms themselves in terms of their product-market scope and the responsibilities of the general manager. We have not as yet addressed in any detail the much more difficult job of the general manager at the corporate level of the multi-business enterprise.

An understanding of the general management task at the corporate level of the diversified firm is clearly helpful to those who aspire to that position themselves. An understanding of these companies and the tasks their managers face is also important to the far greater number who will serve at the many other managerial levels or in staff or specialist capacities in such organizations, and particularly those involved in strategic planning activities at either the business unit or the corporate level.

An understanding of the overall strategic and organizational problems of such firms will also be helpful to those of you who someday hope to act as management consultants or investment bankers to them or to deal with them as suppliers, financial analysts, or loan officers. It is also apparent that those who seek to influence the behavior of such large companies via public policy could also benefit in many cases from a better understanding of the nature of the institution they are trying to regulate or influence.

This chapter will provide some background on the development and the extent of diversification in American industry.[1] The next chapter will describe the additional complexities that strategies of diversification have brought to the general management task at the corporate level in diversified companies. The remaining chapters will develop further the concept of strategy in the diversified firm and show how the framework of analysis you have already developed can be applied to general management problems at the corporate level in the diversified firm as well.

Developing an understanding of the general manager's job in any enterprise is greatly facilitated by trying to imagine yourself in that job and attempting to see the tasks to be done and the context in which they must be accomplished from the viewpoint of the person actually in the job. Most of us are less familiar with the evolution of diversified firms and the nature of the general management tasks at the corporate level in such firms than with single-business companies and product divisions of diversified companies. In order to help you in developing an understanding of the diversified firm, we will next present some background on their development in the United States.

MEASURES OF DIVERSIFICATION

Various measures of diversification have been devised by different researchers, each selecting measures that best fit their interests and the data available to them. Economists interested in the degree of competition in markets and in market structure have tended to relate diversity to the number of different markets in which the firm competes. Economists more interested in issues of firm productivity and specialization have tended to look at diversification in terms of the number of products produced. In both cases, they have tended to use simple and standard measures of product count based on the Standard Industrial Classification (SIC) definitions of product class.

These measures have the great advantage of being easily obtainable from government-required reports and also represent "hard" data in that they are both quantifiable and objective. They have a serious drawback from the perspective of one interested in the management problems of diversification, however. Since they consist of simple counts of products, they cannot take into account the relative importance of the various products in terms of sales, profits, or assets employed. In addition, they assume an equal dissimilarity in the nature of the management task at the product-market level between various SIC product classes. There are also substantial problems arising from the nature of products sometimes included within the same classification, sometimes classified separately.

A less precise but more managerially relevant measure of diversification has been developed by Rumelt.[2] He has developed a set of categories—defined largely in terms of relatedness—designed to capture important differences in both the extent of diversity of a company and in the nature of the managerial relationships among the various businesses of a company. His classification system consists of four mutually exclusive major categories (and eight subcategories) as shown:

1. *Single business:* 95 percent of revenues from largest business unit.
2. *Dominant business:* Between 70 percent and 95 percent of revenues from largest single-business unit.
3. *Related business:* Less than 70 percent of revenues from largest single-business unit, but different from (see No. 4).
4. *Unrelated business:* Also less than 70 percent of revenues from largest single-business unit, but the remainder of the business activities judged to be less related to each other than for the related business category, above.

Rumelt's classifications have been more widely quoted and expanded upon by those interested in the management problems of diversity than the far larger bodies of research based on the study of securities prices or on normative financial models of the firm or the economy. We will return to some of his findings later.

DEGREE OF DIVERSITY

Although uniformly accepted measures of diversification do not exist, the evidence is clear that the extent of diversification in American industry is both high and increasing. Recent estimates place the proportion of the Fortune 500 that are still single-business companies, according to Rumelt's definitions, at about 15 to 20 percent, as shown in Exhibit 10–1. Furthermore, that proportion seems to be continuing to decline.

Since the Fortune 500 firms characteristically account for about two thirds of the industrial output, investment, and employment, and three quarters of the industrial profits in the American economy, the diversified firm is clearly the major and most important form of industrial organization in this country. The same trends toward increasing diversification have occurred in other industrialized economies as well, as is well documented in an article by Scott.[3] If you wish to understand the key managerial activities of the most important firms in the industrialized economies, it is essential to focus on the general management problems at the corporate level of the diversified firm.

EXHIBIT 10–1
Diversification in American Industry

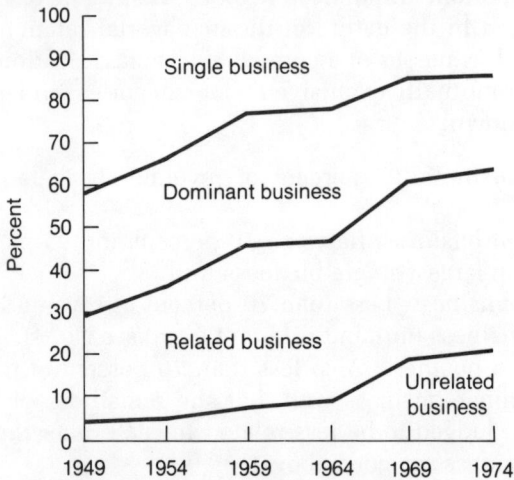

Source: Richard P. Rumelt, "Diversification Strategy
and Profitability", *Strategic Management Journal* 3 (1982),
p. 361. Reprinted by permission of John Wiley & Sons, Ltd.

The trend to diversification began long before the 1949 starting
point of the preceding exhibit, of course. Economists have documented a trend of increasing diversification throughout the history
of American industry. The most managerially relevant study is the
classic *Strategy and Structure* by Alfred Chandler, a leading business historian.[4] Chandler studied in impressive detail the pressures
for diversification and accompanying structural change in General
Motors, Du Pont, Standard Oil of New Jersey, and Sears, Roebuck.
These companies were in the forefront in the 1920s in developing
new administrative structures to cope with the new complexities
brought about by their increasing diversification.

By means of these detailed clinical studies as well as by supporting research in another 70 large enterprises, Chandler explained
convincingly both the pressures that led to diversification as well as
the accompanying changes in organizational structure. The basic
change was to abandon the traditional functional form best suited to
the single business in favor of the now-common product division
form of organization. It was the addition of new activities that invariably resulted in the establishment of product divisions, each with
its own general manager, each painfully created from the existing
functional and highly centralized organizations. It was the creation
of product divisions that in turn created multiple levels of general
management. The problem of determining the most appropriate split

of responsibilities among these various levels unavoidably followed. The desirable degree of decentralization of authority and responsibility from the corporate level to the operating units is a continuing issue in the management of our large companies today.

The substantial diversification that has been taking place in American industry for well over 60 years did not occur smoothly during that period, however. Neither did it occur in the same manner for all companies or for any single company over time.

MAJOR MERGER WAVES

Diversification occurs as a result of some combination of internal development and acquisitions.[5] Information on acquisitions is more readily available to the public than information on diversification from internal sources, and as a result much more analysis has been done on the former than on the latter. Acquisitions have been of great interest to many managers as well as students of business and of public policy, and we will explain briefly some of the major trends that have occurred with regard to merger activity.

Perhaps the least debatable characteristic of mergers is that they seem to come in waves. There is no satisfactory theory to explain or predict these waves of merger activity. In terms of numbers of manufacturing and mining firms acquired, there were distinct peaks around the turn of the century, in the 1920s, in the 1967–70 period, and again in the late 1970s. The first two merger waves are of relatively less interest in terms of contributing significantly to the diversification of American industry since they have been characterized as primarily "merging for monopoly" during the 1887–1904 era and "merging for oligopoly" during the 1919–30 era.

The third merger wave, however, which began in about 1955 but reached its peak in 1968–69, was characterized by a much larger number of conglomerate (neither horizontal nor vertical) mergers. It was estimated by the Federal Trade Commission that about 80 percent of the mergers that occurred during 1948–75 were of the conglomerate type, up very sharply from earlier periods. The peak reached in 1968–69 was high indeed by historical standards. Including firms in manufacturing and mining with assets (acquired) of $10 million or more, the yearly average jumped to almost $13 billion for 1968 and 1969, up from an average of about $3 billion for the preceding 10 years. Almost 10 percent of the total mining and manufacturing assets changed hands during the 1965–70 period, a trend which gave much concern to economists, lawyers, and government agencies interested in concentration and competition in the American economy. In terms of numbers of acquisitions reported, that peaked at about 2,400 in 1970.

In contrast to the earlier merger waves, however, the acquiring firms were no longer the largest companies. In addition, the volume of assets acquired by the larger firms was smaller relative to their size than for medium-sized companies. The contribution to the growth made by merger was therefore more significant to small and medium-sized firms than to the large, and the effects on overall concentration were generally modest.

It was during this period that a number of companies that came to be known as conglomerates expanded rapidly, with growth rates in sales and earnings and stock price that sometimes far outstripped industrial averages. Textron, Litton, and Teledyne are but a few of the many examples of companies that grew rapidly by acquisition during this time, each starting from a very different base, and each pursuing different acquisition strategies to take advantage of the opportunities they encountered or developed.

The conglomerate boom of the late 1960s brought about an extensive investigation of growth via acquisition, since some economists, government agencies, and congressional committees feared that the changes occurring could have permanent and harmful effects on our industrial structure. Indeed, a simple projection of the growth rates experienced by Litton and LTV in the late 1960s would have shown each one of them approaching the total projected GNP for the entire country by 1990.

Critics were also concerned about the increased potential for a number of traditional anticompetitive practices such as predatory pricing, reciprocity, cross-subsidization, and lessened price competition, as well as the social and political implications of the concentration of assets of dissimilar businesses under the control of single corporate managements without any obvious accompanying economic efficiencies. In addition, there was concern that misleading accounting practices were leading investors to overvalue some of these firms, with resulting risk of losses when the inevitable adjustments in valuation occurred.

The frantic merger activity collapsed of its own weight in late 1969, however, several years before an extensive FTC investigation was completed. During this period the investment community had been assigning increasingly high price-earnings (P/E) multiples to companies showing superior growth via acquisition, which in turn made this same continued growth possible. When it became more widely recognized that in many instances a significant part of the gain in reported earnings came from the accounting consequences of the acquisitions rather than from any continuing improvements in operations and that growth by acquisition could not continue at the same rate forever, the P/E multiples declined drastically. As a result, acquisitions based on an exchange of the high P/E stock of the acquirer for the low P/E stock of the target were no longer possible.

The operating troubles and highly leveraged capital structures of some of the companies compounded the problems of conglomerates as a group. The average price-earnings ratio for one sample of 10 large conglomerates fell from 35 at the high point in 1967–68 to well into the single digits in 1970, and the average stock price of the same sample declined by 86 percent in the same short period.[6]

Still a fourth wave of merger activity started in about the middle 1970s, however. Just as other merger waves had differed from each other, in many respects this one as well had some of its own unique characteristics.

Unlike previous merger waves, which had coincided with periods of high stock market prices, this fourth wave developed during a period of depressed prices. There tended to be relatively more large transactions, often involving large, old, and often single-business companies doing the buying. More of the acquisitions involved companies in the service sector than previously. The number of transactions valued at $100 million or more increased steadily from 14 in 1975 to 113 in 1981, and the total value of these large transactions increased from $11.8 billion to $82.6 billion.

The commitment of such large sums of money to acquisitions, whether in the form of cash, exchange of stock, or debt, caused concern on the part of many. Some felt these financial resources would benefit the country more if they were applied to direct investment in physical assets rather than to rearranging the ownership of existing assets. There was, however, no evidence of any significant correlation historically between the total amount of money spent by corporations on direct investment as opposed to acquisitions. Others were concerned that the use of debt by corporations for these purposes would crowd out other private sector borrowers from the capital markets, just as government borrowing crowds out private sector borrowing.

In addition to these concerns over the impact of the merger activity on the financial markets were the more traditional questions of the economic and political effects of the disappearance of independent companies and the consolidation of assets that was taking place. On the political side, it was feared that the large, diversified companies being created so hastily would have more political power than their constituent parts had represented in the past. With regard to economic efficiency, some worried that the new combinations would be less efficient than the individual companies had been before being acquired. Others were just as concerned that the new companies would be so efficient (or predatory) that they would drive out single-business competitors.

Large foreign buyers were increasingly active in the acquisition of American companies. The total dollar value paid for transactions in which a price was reported increased from $3.1 billion in 1977 to $7.1 billion in 1980 and to a record $18.8 billion in 1981. The attraction for the foreign companies was largely the depressed state of the American stock market in relation to earnings and book values, the declining value of the American dollar in terms of foreign currencies, and the judgment that the American economy and political environment provided an attractive long-term investment opportunity. As the dollar strengthened and the American stock market rose dramatically in the fall of 1982, however, the foreign acquisitions declined drastically.

During this fourth merger wave more of the mergers involved cash rather than exchanges in stock, even though the premiums over the pre-merger market price averaged about 50 percent, or about double that of the preceding period. The payment of cash tended to impose a discipline on the merger activity that had been lacking in the earlier conglomerate boom, when a higher proportion of mergers involved the exchange of stock. Without the use of stock as the form of payment, it was no longer possible to achieve an automatic increase in the earnings per share of the acquiring company simply by acquiring a company with a stock selling at a lower price-earnings multiple than that of the acquiring company. The willingness of managements to pay such high cash premiums over the market prices established by individual investors for the same securities raised many questions as to the rationale for such acquisitions, however. As one observer noted, "It takes a lot of confidence in your management ability to justify buying all of a company at a substantial premium over market as opposed to 10 percent of a number of companies at the market price."

Hostile tender offers or takeovers (generally offers to purchase shares made directly to stockholders, without the support of the management of the company to be acquired) also became more common during this period. The common tendencies of managements to resist unexpected and unwanted merger proposals generally resulted in increases in the price of the stock of a company rumored or known to be the subject of an unfriendly takeover bid. This in turn provided great incentives to invest in 5 percent of a company (which would then require a public disclosure under SEC regulations) in the hopes that a bidding war would start. With good planning and a little bit of luck, the original investor could then sell out at a profit as management moved to oppose a possible tender offer and others entered the fray in hopes of a quick profit in the stock. The most consistent winners in the takeover activity were investment bankers and lawyers, however, whose services became much in demand and highly rewarded.

That such hostile takeovers and the large amount of management time and professional fees they consumed contributed anything to the overall productivity of resources in the country or to the wealth of shareholders in total was much less clear. These issues were brought most sharply in focus by the attempt in late 1982 of Bendix to take over the smaller Martin-Marietta Corporation. Martin-Marietta countered by announcing a takeover attempt of Bendix in return, a move described as a "Pac-Man" strategy. At one point it seemed that each corporation might end up owning a majority of the shares of the other, as the shareholders of each company took advantage of the opportunity to tender their shares to the other company at a premium over the market price.

United Technologies, much larger than either Bendix or Martin-Marietta, then announced a plan to enter the battle on the side of the underdog, Martin-Marietta. This prompted Bendix to turn to the Allied Chemical Corporation as a "white knight" to rescue them from the combined counterattack of Martin-Marietta and United Technologies. As the drama—reminiscent of a Gilbert and Sullivan operetta—drew to a close, there was much debate as to who had gained and who had lost in the battle among multibillion-dollar contenders.

United Technologies never did become actively involved and was unaffected by the fray. Martin-Marietta shareholders saw the debt burden of their company increase drastically to almost 90 percent of capitalization as a result of the debt incurred to purchase Bendix shares at a premium during the battle, and lawsuits against their directors followed. If Bendix had been successful in acquiring Martin-Marietta, the debt level of the combined entity would have been higher than originally anticipated as well. Allied shareholders saw their company pay a substantial premium over market price for Bendix in a complicated transaction which also raised the debt level of Allied from 23 percent of capitalization to about 43 percent for the combined entity. The only clear winners in the short term were the Bendix shareholders. They were able to tender their shares to Allied at a premium over the earlier market price premium because their management, which had started it all, lost its battle to acquire Martin-Marietta and turned to Allied to avoid being taken over by the combination of United Technologies and Martin-Marietta.

Coming as it did within a year of the largest merger in history and one of the most controversial in recent times—that of the Du Pont takeover (for about $7 billion) of Conoco as the latter sought to escape a takeover bid by Seagram's—the Bendix battle caused an unprecedented amount of attention to the common sense of such activities. It was clear that the outcome of such battles was influenced strongly by the personal ambitions of the managers involved and the short-term financial interests of whoever happened to own the stock, even though they might have bought it yesterday and might sell it tomorrow for a quick profit. Merger and acquisition specialists and lawyers specializing in merger tactics (sometimes referred to as the "Strike Bar") benefited greatly, regardless of the outcome of such battles.

The relationship between a corporate strategy based on product-market factors or the distinctive business competences of the companies involved and the outcome of these battles, however, was less clear. The ultimate decisions concerning the long-term restructuring of major corporations seemed to be affected strongly by parties that had little concern for and no continuing interest in the performance of the surviving enterprises. It seemed to many that managerial ambitions and financial opportunism were displacing industrial logic to an unprecedented degree.

Our concern in this text is with the formulation and implementation of strategy from the general manager's point of view in the ongoing business organization. Diversification via acquisition is certainly an important and legitimate aspect of corporate strategy. Shareholders and society both would likely be less concerned about some of the recent major mergers, however, if they felt the motives behind such expansion were based more on industrial logic than on seeking growth by taking advantage of the ability to offer an immediate profit to the shareholders of the target company in return for their shares. Some of the takeover activity of this fourth merger wave has brought forth renewed interest in the governance of corporations, a matter sure to be of increasing importance in the decade ahead.

INTERNAL DEVELOPMENT

Accompanying all of this acquisition activity, but receiving less attention because the efforts are not subject to public reporting in the same manner as acquisitions, has been the historic pattern of growth through internal development mentioned earlier.

Diversification via internal development is obviously a much slower process than by acquisition, and one which is likely to lead the company into areas much more closely related to its present businesses than diversification via acquisition. It is not necessarily a preferred route. That it has not been an easy or profitable one for many companies has been well documented by Biggadike, who found that it takes an average of eight years for internal ventures to become profitable.[7] Fast, looking at the success and longevity of new venture divisions in large corporations (divisions formed for the purpose of starting a number of new ventures, not just a single new venture) found similar difficulties and frustrations for managers charged with the task of developing new ventures internally.[8]

Although precise comparisons are impossible because of the lack of data, diversification via internal development appears to have had an effect on our industrial economy comparable to that resulting from mergers. A number of our older, highly diversified companies, such as General Electric and Westinghouse, although active in the early merger waves, expanded into new product areas largely though the commercialization of developments from their research laboratories and the internal expansion of existing product or market capabilities. Their diversification strategy was quite different from that of the conglomerates and took longer to accomplish. The end result of diversification by both acquisition and internal development has been the same, however. We now have an economy in which the large company concentrating its resources on a single line or even a few lines of business is clearly the exception.

ECONOMIC EFFECTS

Two important questions are what the economic effects of all this acquisition and diversification have been with regard to the performance of the firm and the returns to investors. If certain strategies of diversification seem to lead to better economic performance than others, that would certainly be useful for managers to know. Generalizations based on research and applicable to the specific situation would be a most welcome addition to the analytical arsenal of the manager considering diversification.

This is an area in which academic researchers have been much interested, and a great amount of research has been done over the last decade or so[9]. Extensive work has been done to find correlations between the degree of diversification and/or acquisition activity and performance measures such as return on capital or equity or total return to holders of the common stock. A number of these studies are summarized in the references listed in footnote 9.

Mergers obviously contribute to the growth in sales of the acquiring firm in the year of the merger. The degree to which mergers contribute to either the growth or the profitability of the acquiring firms over a longer period of time is much less clear, however; the evidence is somewhat contradictory and, on balance, inconclusive. It is clear that the stockholders of the acquired firm benefit in the short run from being acquired, simply because of the premium over market price invariably paid. Studies which have attempted to relate either corporate profitability or total return to investors to the number of acquisitions or to overall measures of diversity of the parent company, however, have generally found no significant relationships. A recent exception is a study by Asquith et al. which did find that the shareholders of bidding firms do benefit very modestly from the activity.[10] One of the few issues on which witnesses at periodic congressional hearings on mergers generally have agreed upon to date, however, is that the evidence with regard to the economic effect of mergers is inconclusive. In any event, aggregate empirical studies such as described above provide little guidance as yet for the manager concerned with whether or how his firm should diversify.

Rumelt's study, referred to earlier, did find significant variations in profitability when firms were grouped into his categories rather than by degree of diversification based on product counts or by the amount of acquisition activity. Working with a random sample of 273 companies from the Fortune 500 list, he showed, among other things, that strategies of related diversification in general were associated with superior economic performance, and that the worst category was the "passive-unrelated" one.

With regard to the managerial implications of these findings, however, it is far less clear that the different strategies were in themselves the *cause* of the ensuing performances. The industries the companies were in, and therefore also able to enter most easily, played an important role both in the diversification strategies chosen and in the subsequent profitability, as he showed in later research.[11]

High-profit industries tend to have high barriers to entry in the form of the technology or the investment required. A strategy of related diversification is therefore most appropriate for a company in such an industry if there is an opportunity to enter related industries with the similar characteristics of high entry barriers and high profits. This is what many companies in that fortunate position have quite properly chosen to do. As a result, at least a part of the reason a strategy of related diversification ends up in Rumelt's high-performance classification is that those for whom such a strategy is best, namely companies already in a high-profit industry with the opportunity to diversify into related fields, are the companies most likely to follow that strategy. It does not follow that a strategy of related diversification is preferable for a company faced with low profitability, for whatever reason, in their own industry as well as closely related industries.

A typical example of an attempt to follow a strategy of related diversification can be seen in the origins of the Sybron Company of Rochester, New York, now a corporation approaching sales of a billion dollars. The original Pfaudler Company (about $15 million sales in 1953) had a dominant share of the slowly growing, cyclical, and technically vulnerable worldwide market for glass-lined steel tanks. An unsolicited offer to purchase the company forced a decision between being acquired, continuing their slow and cyclical (although profitable) growth, or striking out in new areas on their own. Numerous activities closely related in terms of technology, products, or markets had been explored and either rejected or tried without success. As a result, the company ended up diversifying by acquisition into less related fields.

The dilemma is that related diversification, about which a company may know the most and for which it has the most relevant skills, may not solve its basic problems. Unrelated diversification, however, lying at the other end of the spectrum of activities a company may choose to enter, presents substantially greater challenges of evaluation and management. Unfortunately, the aggregate financial research that has been done to date provides little, if any, direct guidance to the general manager concerned with developing a strategy of diversification for his specific company. As a general manager, you will have to be concerned not just with correlations but also with cause-and-effect relationships that may help you improve your specific situation.

Apparent, however, is the considerable variation over long periods of time in the performance of diversified companies; some consistently perform significantly better than others. In addition, there is evidence that some single-business companies have been able to improve their growth and profits by means of diversification. Your challenge as a manager is to combine the limited help available from the aggregate empirical research with an analytical approach to the problems and potential of your specific situation to develop a plan that improves upon what otherwise would have happened.

MERGER AND DIVERSIFICATION MOTIVES

Much has been written about the motives of management which have led to such a clear and pronounced trend away from concentration on a single line of business. The search for such motives has been heightened by the fact that neither traditional arguments pointing out the advantages of economies of scale and a large market share in the single product line, financial theory, nor empirical financial research provide satisfactory explanations for the observed trends of diversification and acquisition activity. Financial theorists in particular frequently make the argument that shareholders would benefit if companies would distribute any financial resources that cannot be usefully employed in their existing businesses to their shareholders rather than use it for diversification efforts. The shareholders could then reinvest these proceeds as they see fit, they argue, choosing the type and extent of diversification they wish to have in their portfolio themselves.

Underlying motives for any action are always difficult to prove;

only the resulting actions are directly observable. It seems apparent, however, that the underlying reasons for diversification have been the desires of management for some combination of increased growth, profits, and stability for the firm. Chandler found that diversification occurred historically when companies had accumulated resources in excess of what was needed to fully exploit their historic lines of business and then applied these resources to new fields of endeavor in order to continue their growth. He noted that organizations, just as individuals, develop goals of their own, and in healthy organizations these goals include stability and continued growth.

Paul Davies, then chairman of FMC Corporation, a large company which diversified aggressively in the late 1950s, stated his reasons very simply: "To make sure everything doesn't go to hell at once." Royal Little, the founder of Textron, frequently justified his wide-ranging diversification efforts as a way of constantly redeploying assets from areas of lower return to higher return in order to earn the highest possible profits for the stockholders. Akito Morita, president of Sony of Japan, stated that his principal reason for engaging in a widespread diversification effort in the early 80s was to provide a variety of interesting jobs for his managers as their interests and abilities changed, as it was customary for them to remain with the company for life. Litton executives often justified their ambitious acquisition program in terms of the benefits to be gained from combining new technologies with existing businesses to achieve dramatic rather than incremental commercial advantages. Many firms have cited the advantages of size and increased stability of earnings as justification for acquisitions.

Just because countless business executives have repeated these themes in one variation or another in explaining their actions does not mean that personal ambitions are not also involved, that the actions will always turn out to have been in the stockholder's interest, or that the manager's and the stockholder's interests are always congruent. As in all fields of human endeavor, motives are mixed and not always clear, and results are not always as hoped for. To consider the motives we have suggested as being important, however, is a useful starting point.

It is clear that nonbusiness organizations as well often seem to be guided by similar goals. It is not unheard of for military units, government agencies, or congressional staffs to aggressively seek larger budgets and broader mandates. Even the highly respected March of Dimes charity, first started when Franklin Delano Roosevelt was president, changed its goals from the prevention and treatment of polio to research on and treatment of congenital birth defects when the development of the Salk vaccine effectively put the original March of Dimes out of business.

You can usefully think of the great trend to diversification, then, as arising largely from the natural and widespread desire of managements to make use of excess or obtainable resources in order to take advantage of an opportunity or to solve a problem. Although this may describe managerial motives in broad terms, you will surely want to look carefully at each situation you encounter to discern just what that particular management was trying to accomplish and how they went about it. That the motives that lead various managements to diversify may have much in common at the general level of a desire for some combination of increased stability, growth, and profits in no way lessens the need to look carefully at the reasons for diversifying in the individual situation.

The trend to diversification can be thought of in even broader terms. It is another example of the increasing professionalization of management which has occurred since World War II, at first in the United States and now elsewhere. Just as the corporate form of management provides a means to efficiently extend the life cycle of the single business beyond the lifetime of the individual owners, the strategy of diversification represents a means to extend the life cycle of the corporation beyond the hazards and limitations of the single industry. The development of management skills which transcend specific industries has made diversification feasible.

SUMMARY

The key issue for the general manager is not whether certain generic diversification strategies seem to be associated with high or low returns on average. As a general manager, you will be primarily concerned with developing strategies that are likely to present a solution to the problems, opportunities, and aspirations of your particular company. You will need to be concerned with cause-and-effect relationships, not just correlations, and with your specific company, not just companies in general. Increasing the stability of earnings or improving the growth or profitability of a company over time by means of diversifying into areas of more promise represents a substantial accomplishment to most business executives, and they are objectives which explain much diversification activity.

CHAPTER 11

New Tasks and Complexities

In the last chapter we noted the long-term major trend to diversification in American industry. In this chapter we will be more explicit about the new tasks and added complexities that general managers face as a result of diversification.

LEVELS OF GENERAL MANAGEMENT

Historically, we have tended to think of the general manager as the executive to whom the functional managers report. The job evolved in this manner, and much of the literature, research, and teaching on management historically has made the implicit, if not explicit, assumption that general managers are responsible for a single business in an identifiable market and have the assistance of a number of functional managers in marketing, production, finance, and so on, to help them do what they cannot do all by themselves. Indeed, one of the essential tasks of general managers is often described as coordinating the activities of their functional managers in the achievement of the product-market strategy of the firm, an activity for which they are principally—but not solely—responsible. A conceptual framework which focuses on typical single-business tasks is useful in understanding the job of the general manager in the single-product company or in divisions in the middle of larger organizations.

Such a conception of the general manager's position is inaccurate for the higher levels of general management in virtually all of our larger corporations. The trend to diversification and therefore divisionalization and decentralization has created several new layers of general management above the traditional manager of the single business. General managers in diversified firms may have subordinates who as division managers are responsible for businesses with many product lines and hundreds of millions of dollars in sales volume.

There is a clear relationship between this increasing managerial complexity, brought on by strategies of product diversification, and the movement to the product division form of organization, brought on by the attempts to deal with this increasing complexity. The new organizational positions and levels created by the movement to product divisions present different challenges than the old positions and structure, which best served the needs of the single-business organization. In graphic terms, the changes in organizational structure that typically follow a strategy of diversification are as shown in Exhibit 11–1.

What Chandler described so well are the difficulties that companies encountered in trying to administer a number of different products by means of the single functional organization.[1] The natural tendency, as new activities were added to the traditional business, was first to assign responsibility for the various functions of the new and different businesses to the well-established functional departments that already existed. The difficulties for the functional managers in the core business in understanding and managing the functional activities in the new businesses increased rapidly as new activities were added. The eventual solution of having separate businesses report to a new and higher level of general management evolved from the traditional structure of having all functional units report directly to the top management of the company.

An intermediate step is often followed as companies add new activities to an existing predominantly single-business operation. Instead of moving directly to the product division form of organization, companies often make a more gradual transition by retaining the functional organization for the original core of the business, but organizing the new activities as separate business units reporting directly to the existing corporate management. For a variety of reasons such a structure generally evolves into the product division form of organization.

An additional refinement of the typical product division form of organization that has arisen in the diversified company is the creation of strategic business units, or SBUs. As explained in an excellent article by Hall, an SBU is a grouping of assets, people, and products that is useful to treat as a unit for strategic planning purposes.[2] Such groupings often coincide with divisions, but in the larger diversified companies with divisions more closely related to each other or stemming from a common technology, SBUs can be

EXHIBIT 11–1
Multi-Business Organization Chart

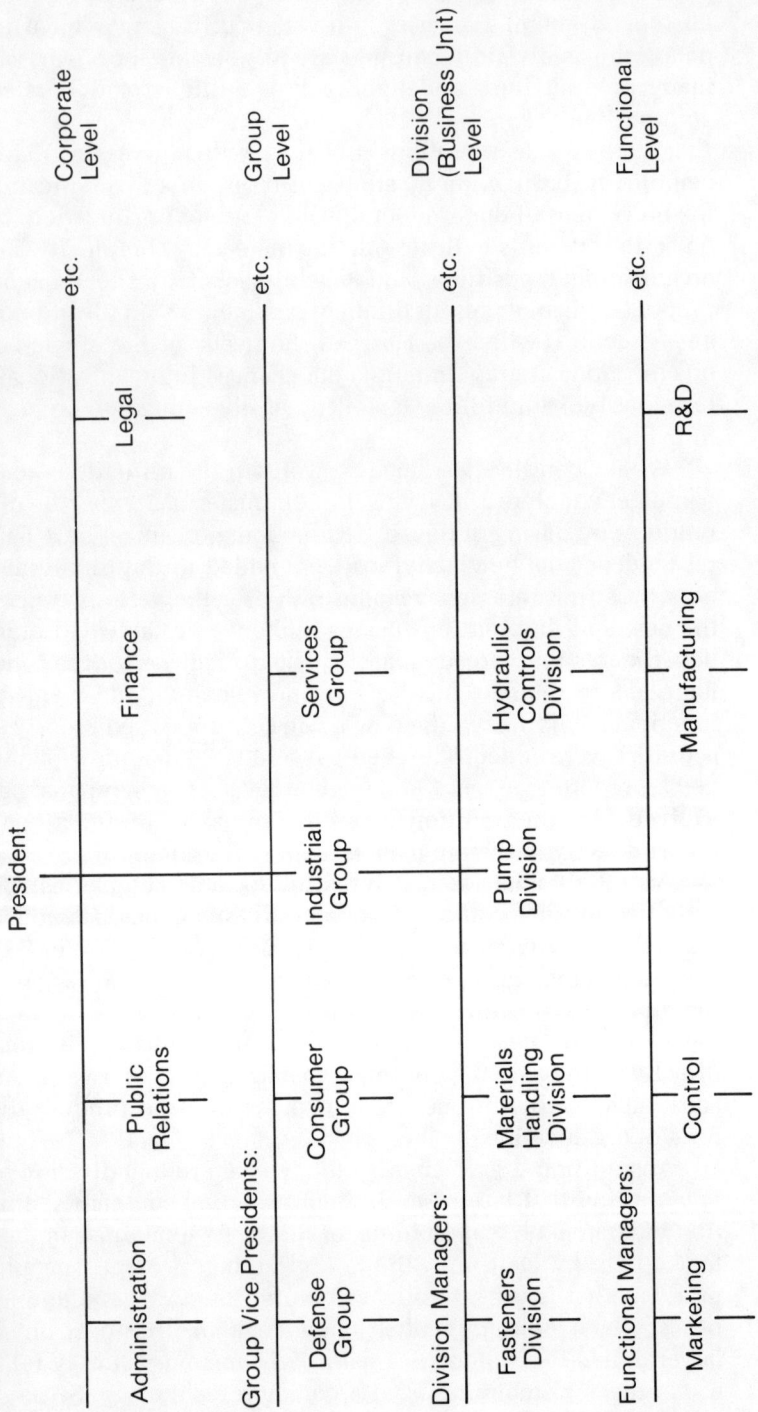

President

Administration   Public Relations   Finance   Legal   etc.   Corporate Level

Group Vice Presidents:

Defense Group   Consumer Group   Industrial Group   Services Group   etc.   Group Level

Division Managers:

Fasteners Division   Materials Handling Division   Pump Division   Hydraulic Controls Division   etc.   Division (Business Unit) Level

Functional Managers:

Marketing   Control   Manufacturing   R&D   etc.   Functional Level quite different from the divisional organization. In some cases a division will contain several SBUs; in other cases, several divisions (or portions of them) can most usefully be thought of as a single SBU.

The General Electric Company in the 1950–80 period provides an excellent example of the continual changes in organizational structure and approach to strategic planning that can occur as companies try to find better ways to deal with the management of diversity.[3] The company, with sales of about $26 billion in 1982, is presently one of the most diversified in the country, competing in 23 of the 26 two-digit SIC industry categories. It has long been regarded as a very well-managed company and has in particular been regarded as a leader in the development of strategic planning systems and techniques.

General Electric was a highly centralized and largely functionally organized company when Ralph Cordiner became president in 1950. Cordiner led a massive decentralization of the company into units "of a size that a man could get his arms around." These units were designated as *departments* in GE, but they would commonly be called *divisions* in most companies. By the early 1960s GE had been reorganized into five groups consisting of 25 divisions which in turn consisted of 190 departments, each with much more authority than before to function as independent business units.

Evaluating the strategy and operations of 190 separate businesses is of course an overwhelming task for the top management, and so different groupings and approaches continued to evolve. Because of the difficulty of evaluating the departments separately and a dissatisfaction with the grouping of the 190 or so departments into 25 divisions for strategic planning purposes, Fred Borch (president from 1963 to 1972) created, as a result of recommendations from the consulting group of McKinsey & Co., 43 SBUs which "overlaid" the department and divisional structure.

There was a substantial build-up of corporate planning staff following the creation of the SBU structure, as more formalized and analytical approaches to strategic planning became popular and corporate management sought help in evaluating the performance and plans of the SBUs. This trend continued under Reginald Jones (1972–81), and Jones introduced several new groupings—sectors and arenas—to assist corporate management in managing the present businesses and identifying new opportunities better.

When Jack Welch became president in 1981, he felt that the corporate management had gotten too far away from understanding and dealing with the businesses at the SBU level, partly by concentrating on the larger aggregations of businesses and partly because of the increasing reliance on strategic planning staffs at all levels and the formalization of planning that had occurred. He announced a drastic cutback in the 200 or so strategic planners employed at all levels, a concentration on evaluation by line management of business performance and prospects at the SBU level, and an emphasis on finding and supporting entrepreneurs within the organization.[4]

Within a period of about 30 years, then, GE went through a period of decentralization followed by an increasing aggregation of business units, build-up of staff to assist line management in their tasks, formalization of procedures, and then a reversal of direction at the end of the period. The changes were in response to the challenges of managing such a diversified company and represented a continual willingness to try new approaches as the shortcomings of the existing approaches became more troublesome.

General Electric is but one example of how the existence of many businesses and organizational levels in the diversified company makes the job of the general manager or president of the traditional single-business company in many ways more like the job of the general manager of a division, rather than that of the president, in a diversified company. The division manager, not the corporate president, is responsible for specific products and the supervision of the functional departments. The division manager has to know or learn a great deal about the products and markets he is responsible for and the organization that has been built up over time to serve those markets. The group vice president, and surely the president, cannot possibly have as great a degree of familiarity with all of the many businesses under their control.

The demands placed on the top managers of diversified companies are not only complex but also different. As diversity increases, these demands would at some point seem to exceed the capacities of both people and organizations to deal with them effectively. Responsibility and power become increasingly removed from the reality of the business operations and the people running them. The connecting links between the operating businesses and the corporate level increasingly become quantitative reports, written summaries, conferences, staff assistants, and more abstract models of the various businesses and their environments. Economists and social scientists discuss the problem in terms of the managerial inefficiencies which appear to accompany increased size and diversity and which they believe must ultimately negate whatever other economic advantages growth via diversification might bring to the organization. Lammot Copeland, when he was president of Du Pont, stated his opinion in a more direct way: "Running a conglomerate is a job for management geniuses, not ordinary mortals such as we at Du Pont."

INCREASED STRATEGIC OPTIONS

The most dramatic new task which ordinary mortals must nevertheless master arises from the fact that both present and potential strategic options of the firm have by definition been broadened considerably. The manager of the diversified firm (or the firm considering diversification) can no longer be concerned only with the problems and prospects of a single business. He will not have the time to become deeply involved in the development of strategy for very many of the individual businesses or in the allocation of resources to various functional areas and programs in support of specific business strategies. The manager must now make, or at least assume responsibility for, decisions about which products and markets to compete in—not just how to compete in given product markets.

The fundamental notion of "our industry" obviously loses its meaning as the company diversifies. For the highly diversified company it becomes almost meaningless in the traditional product-market sense. The more a company diversifies, the less attention the manager can pay to any one industry, and the more the manager will be forced to rely on the judgments of others or on abstractions which try to capture the important characteristics of an industry for someone who is not intimately familiar with it. This may be useful in that it can provide a broader look across a number of industries than might otherwise be possible. An unavoidable shortcoming, however, is the loss of the ability to be as close to the trends and people and happenings of a specific industry as any good operating manager should be.

The new and critical strategic choice that faces the general manager at the corporate level, then, becomes the selection of products and markets in which to engage and the development of both a rationale for that particular choice as well as a means of making that choice effective. Although general managers of diversified firms can no longer be primarily concerned with the development of strategy for a single business, neither can they ignore the strategic position and performance of their existing units as they consider the broader issues of the product-market portfolio. Therein lies a substantial dilemma, to which we shall return later.

This enlarged strategic horizon for the firm complicates the job of the general manager in the search and evaluation of new activities. Without a managerially oriented rationale for what businesses to consider, you would be faced with the prospect of investigating the whole world of business activity in pursuit of opportunities suitable for your specific situation or else reacting on a case-by-case basis to opportunities as they arise. Neither of these extreme approaches is likely to seem suitable to the manager not only committed to an analytical approach, but also to action within reasonable limits of thought and investigation. The development of such guidelines is not easy for the individual company. If they permit the firm to go beyond its present businesses, as is their purpose, someone will have to understand the opportunities that exist for that specific company in new products and markets.

Questions of the divestment of existing operations—a necessary option to consider if one is to view the products and divisions of a company as elements of a portfolio—may not be as difficult analytically because of the greater familiarity with any operation which has been a part of the company. The analytical benefits the manager gains because of greater familiarity are no doubt more than offset by the administrative difficulties of selling an existing operation, however, as well as the unavoidable need to consider the effects of the divestment of an ailing division on the reported earnings of the company and the people that will be affected by the sale.

ALLOCATION OF RESOURCES TO OPERATIONS

Additions to and deletions from the portfolio of a corporation are dramatic but (for most companies) periodic and perhaps infrequent major resource allocation decisions. The allocation of resources to the various subunits of the corporation is another new and continuing task, however, influenced by every budget, capital appropriation request, incentive plan, and profit goal from each division. The question is no longer the allocation of resources among the functional departments of a single business, with some requirements of balance among the departments in order to achieve the overall goals of the business. Instead, the corporate level now has the task of channeling financial resources from one division to another in accordance with their perception of the best opportunities for spending the corporation's limited resources. The old challenge of allocating resources to their most productive use is raised to the level of choosing among separate and often dissimilar businesses. In broad terms this can be described as substituting an internal capital market for the traditional external capital markets.

Allocating resources is a task the corporate level can in no way avoid since even objective decision rules, profit goals, or capital hurdle rates will influence the pattern of cash flows into or out of divisions. From the corporate point of view, there is no reason to assume that the divisions with the highest current cash flow or profits are also those which should have the most money to spend on their own futures. Neither is there any reason to believe that the establishment of uniform profit goals for all divisions, or the establishment of incentive plans which are based on individual division profits, will result in the best allocation of resources in view of the long-term objectives and opportunities for the entire corporation. Finally, any attempt to allocate resources primarily on the basis of a companywide ranking of the rates of return of individual investment proposals encounters significant problems with regard to the possible bias or provincialism of the proposals, the likely interdependence of proposals with each other and other activities, and the inability of the corporate level to understand in any great depth many diverse proposals.

The objective is not just to evaluate each division's plans on its own merits but to evaluate each relative to the others. This poses very considerable analytical and administrative problems. A thorough review of a division cannot be done quickly or frequently. If the goal is to evaluate the opportunities facing any one division in relation to the opportunities in all of the divisions, however, it is necessary to have the reviews close enough together so that comparisons can be made and remembered before the decisions are final. Analogies which compare the virtually instantaneous analysis of a large sample of common stocks to construct the most efficient investment portfolio, based as they are on computer processing of large amounts of readily available quantified data, are of little help for this substantial managerial task.

The more the corporate level seeks to actively influence the allocation of funds among the divisions, the more someone at the corporate level must make trade-offs among unlike and little-known alternatives. Influencing the content of the strategies at the division level is even more difficult, as it involves exercising judgment with regard to products, markets, and an organization in a situation where division management is certain to have more knowledge than corporate management.

It may be that no one of these problems of resource allocation is different in principle than the traditional single-business problems more familiar to all of us. Adding greatly to the number of problems and the different industry settings in which they occur, however, creates a formidable intellectual and administrative task. It is further complicated by the fact that the various levels and units in the organization have different interests, perspectives, and biases. Obtaining commonly accepted and objective data—whether historical data or forecasts and judgments—is not always easy. The past can be as difficult to interpret as the future is uncertain.

In addition, just because a company adopts the product division form of organization, it does not follow that the strategy and operations of each division are necessarily independent of all of the other divisions except for the allocation of financial resources. Depending on the nature of the businesses of the various divisions and on the approach of the corporate level to the relationships among the divisions, there may be numerous opportunities or even requirements for the coordination of research and development, manufacturing, or marketing activities of divisions with each other. Some companies prefer to let the self-interests of the individual divisions govern such matters; others prefer to play a more active role. In either event, interrelationships complicate the strategic evaluations and the allocation of resources.

MANAGING MANAGERS

A third task that arises for the chief executive in the diversified corporation is the training, selection, evaluation, motivation, and reward of general managers (division presidents) rather than functional specialists (vice presidents of manufacturing, marketing, finance, and so on).

The job of the general manager of the single business is more complex in many ways than that of his functional subordinates in that it involves both variables and more complex variables than most functional responsibilities entail. In addition, the impact of many of the general manager's most important decisions can best be measured in terms of several years or even decades; functional decisions and managers can usually be evaluated over a shorter period of time. One can of course evaluate a division manager very largely on "the bottom line" every month or quarter, but that entails many long-run risks and costs.

The general manager at the corporate level of the diversified company has to understand the performance and the potential of division managers of businesses different from each other and located physically away from headquarters. It will also be important to assess the quality and potential of the managers at lower levels within the division. Both of these tasks are more difficult than that faced by a division president in evaluating the six or so functional managers that report directly to him, where he has likely known them for a longer period of time and they are all in the same industry, organization, and (probably) location.

CORPORATE-LEVEL STRATEGY

The fourth new task is to develop a strategy which is useful for the corporation as a whole and which is something more than the sum of the division strategies. The president of the diversified company has among his tasks that of defining and communicating just what the "central theme," "core skills," "business mission," or "concept of the corporation" are in operational terms that go beyond the ones that describe the single-product firm competing in the single industry. Developing a statement of strategy for the diversified firm that is a useful guide to action for those within the firm, and not just an attractive statement for outside consumption, is a most challenging intellectual exercise. The next chapter will explore in more detail the concept of corporate strategy as it must be modified to be useful at the corporate level of the diversified firm.

SUMMARY

New problems always prompt the development of new tools, techniques, conceptual schemes, and organizational arrangements to deal with them. So it is with diversification. Divisionalization and decentralization were the basic solutions to the managerial problems created by product diversity, which was in itself a response to other problems and opportunities. As managements gained experience in the management of diversity, refinements such as product groups, sectors, SBUs, and numerous analytical techniques and models followed. These developments all contributed to the creation of new jobs at the corporate and group levels as well as to the redefinition of the general manager's job at the division level.

Many years ago the development of the teaching area of Business Policy represented a jump in the level of abstraction from that of the specialist and the functional manager to the generalist responsible for the enterprise as a whole. In some ways we now have similar adjustments to make in our thinking about these new levels of general management created in the diversified company.

It is unfortunate but unavoidable that as the territory becomes more complex and the problems to be dealt with more numerous, as is the case as a company diversifies, the president is forced to view the territory from increasingly higher levels of abstraction. At the same time that we are proudly adding layers to the beehive and constructing all kinds of elaborate tunnels within it, the queen bee is becoming more and more removed from the workers and their daily forays for pollen. But it is at the operating level that the products or services are generated and the income received. As an experienced division manager in one highly diversified company remarked:

> We have got to keep in mind what makes the corporation go. It isn't headquarters; I never have seen a headquarters that generated income by itself. The foundation for the whole operation is in the divisions; it is in the divisions that the money is spent and the money is earned.

That is mainly where we have to worry about selling things for more than they cost to make. Headquarters, of course, has an important role to play, but it is too easy for them to get preoccupied with their own needs.[5]

After exploring in more detail the nature of corporate strategy in the diversified firm in the next chapter, we will then deal with the development of the role of the headquarters in subsequent chapters.

CHAPTER 12

Corporate Strategy in the Diversified Firm

In this chapter we will suggest how the concept of strategy as developed for the single-business company can be expanded to make it applicable to the corporate level of the diversified company as well.

LEVELS OF STRATEGY

The basic factors which complicate the application of a concept of strategy developed for the single business to the corporate level of the diversified firm are the existence of many products and markets, not just one, and several levels of general management. In the single-business firm, *strategy* and *corporate strategy* are used interchangeably and describe the means by which the firm has chosen to compete in their primary product and market. In the multi-business firm there will be at least two levels of organizational units—the corporate level and the business level—for which the concept of strategy' is applicable. The key fact that you should keep in mind is that traditional product-market strategies exist primarily at the business (or SBU) level in all companies. The strategies at higher levels in the organization must encompass those lower business-level strategies as well as additional considerations relevant to the new levels, and that is what complicates the matter.

In the diversified company the corporate level has responsibility for a number of businesses as well as for the traditional financial, legal, and administrative tasks common to all corporations. Product groups—organizational units made up of several divisions—are an intermediate level between the business and the corporate levels. Some companies (such as General Electric, as described in the last chapter) have created additional organizational levels such as sectors and arenas that can also be charged with developing and implementing a strategy. Strategic business units often coincide with divisions; but in the larger corporation they often consist of several divisions or parts of divisions. True product-market strategies exist primarily at the business level, however, and that is where the general managers and the functional organizations responsible for a traditional business are located.

In Chapter 2 we suggested that a statement of strategy

> should convey both what a company is trying to achieve and how it hopes to achieve it. The plan for achievement should include attention to the important factors influencing that achievement, as mentioned, and it should specify what major steps are to be taken, in what rough time frame, by whom, what resources will be required, and how the resources will be obtained. It should communicate, in as tangible a way as possible, just how this particular company has chosen to compete in the marketplace.

That general prescription applies to the corporate level as well as to the business level. The corporate level, however, now has to be concerned with what businesses to compete in, as well as how, and with what resources to devote to the many businesses in which it is presently engaged. It is important for the manager of the single business to be familiar with the specific products, markets, competitors, and functional policies of that business, as we have emphasized. At the corporate level in the diversified company, comparable knowledge and involvement is not possible. The corporation, however, still needs to have its own objectives and plans for achieving them. These objectives and plans unavoidably influence and in turn depend upon the strategies of the individual divisions. A corporate-level strategy that is unrelated to division strategies, skills, and opportunities is not very useful. Neither is a corporate strategy that is simply a listing of the various division strategies and product lines.

A business-level strategy can be thought of as an organizing concept that helps relate the activities of the functional departments to the opportunities in the external environment for the single business. The corporate strategy in the multi-business corporation can be thought of as the organizing concept which both explains and guides the activities of the many separate businesses within the corporation. Business-level strategies deal with the plans for spending money by functional departments in a given product-market area. Corporate strategy in the diversified company is more concerned with how much the corporation should spend in both present and potential product-market areas and why. Neither level can develop its strategy independently of the other.

Some argue that the overall corporate strategy in the diversified firm can and should be nothing more than the summation of the product-market opportunities and strategic plans at the business-unit level. In this view, the role of the corporate level is largely to assign priorities to divisional claims on the limited corporate resources, allocating money according to the attractiveness of divisional capital investment and spending proposals. This is the logical extension of financial theory and capital-budgeting procedures, in which capital should be allocated to the most promising uses as long as the returns projected exceed the firm's cost of capital. The firm's overall strategy and lines of business are then simply the result of a number of individual spending decisions. The need to have a broader, corporate-level strategy that can provide guidance for the corporate level and be communicated to the divisions for use by them in devising their plans becomes, like the concept of the soul to an atheist, far less important.

There are substantial analytical difficulties in determining relevant cash flows, time periods, and discount rates under the best of circumstances. It is even more difficult in the large corporation to secure project proposals that are completely independent of other proposals and activities and sufficiently free from natural enthusiasm, limited horizons, and perhaps even a little deliberate bias. When the number of significant projects that must be dealt with number in the many hundreds or even thousands, as is the case in the larger corporations, the task becomes even more difficult. As a result, the corporate level, which is responsible for many businesses but far removed from any individual business, is likely to find it uncomfortable to base the entire corporate strategy on such an allocation process.

There is a more serious disadvantage to viewing the corporate role in the determination of strategy as little more than an allocator of funds to competing uses. We will turn next to the issue of the unique skills or distinctive competence of the corporation.

DISTINCTIVE COMPETENCE

A view more commonly held by managers, and one which we support, is that even the most diversified company needs a broader conception of itself than simply an allocator of resources to the most promising opportunities that arise. In deciding what businesses to compete in and how to compete in them, attention must be paid to what the resources and skills of the *overall* corporation are and how these can be most effectively utilized in the accomplishment of an overall corporate purpose. If there is little attention paid to why that particular corporation should have an advantage in pursuing certain kinds of market opportunity or little effort made to influence what is proposed so as to take advantage of such corporate skills, superior performance is unlikely to result. A business strategy based on some concept of distinctive competence and the pursuit of specified opportunities is just as important for the corporate level in the diversified company as for the individual division or independent company.

Identifying and developing such distinctive competences for the corporate level of the diversified firm is far more difficult than the comparable task for the single-business firm, where the strengths are much more likely to be defined in relation to specific products and markets. In the diversified firm, distinctive strengths will generally have to be stated at a higher level of abstraction.

Litton Industries, for example, during its period of high growth and numerous acquisitions, was explicit about its belief that it had distinctive skills in conceptualizing and commercializing new business opportunities based on the combination of state-of-the-art electronic technology, often from the defense industry, with existing products and markets. Textron, during a similar phase in its corporate history, saw itself as having very different skills. Textron concentrated largely on the acquisition of manufacturing companies for which capital and generalized management skills, its principal corporate resources, could make a difference in the competitive position of the divisions. Both Westinghouse and General Electric during much of their history followed still a different course building upon their core research, manufacturing, and marketing skills to concentrate on products that generate, control, or use electricity.

All of the above companies made significant moves during the past decade into businesses seemingly unrelated to the above distinctive competences. Litton, for example, became involved in projects as diverse as economic development contracts in Greece and the restaurant business in the United States; Textron acquired an insurance company; Westinghouse entered the modular housing industry on a large scale; and General Electric made a major investment in learning systems and educational services. More recently most of these companies have been moving back to a product strategy based on a more limited definition of the distinctive strengths of the corporation, as many of the radically new ventures did not turn out as well as hoped. In the case of General Electric, there is also now a determined effort to move beyond the relatively mature electro-mechanical technologies of many of the present businesses, partly by means of an emphasis by the new president on developing a much stronger entrepreneurial atmosphere within the company.

The point is not that companies should not occasionally try to move into activities beyond those that seemingly would benefit from the application of the demonstrated distinctive competences of the corporation or that ventures which do fit well with those competences always turn out well. It is the attempt to develop and build on *some* distinctive corporate strength that is important. Without that, any corporation, as Alfred Sloan put it, is simply "chasing after some lucky star."

It is clear that most of the product-market components of the concept of strategy that are useful at the business level are far less relevant at the corporate level in the diversified company. Other factors change as well, as described below.

LONG-TERM FINANCIAL GOALS

The concept of strategy at the corporate level in the diversified company should address long-term growth and profitability goals, just as in the single-business company. The derivation of these may range from somewhat arbitrarily selected goals arrived at by a "top-down" process to a consolidation of the plans submitted by the existing units, adjusted downward through experience or conservatism, or upward as a form of encouragement or pressure.

The overall financial objectives are not as readily derived from conditions in the existing businesses as in the single-business company, however, since the limitations of any single industry do not apply. Indeed, it is the desire to avoid the constraints arising from the conditions in a single industry that often causes companies to seek profits and growth elsewhere. It should be apparent, however, that just because the pharmaceutical industry has for decades ranked at or near the top of all industries in return on equity or because Xerox or IBM or McDonald's have been highly profitable and growing companies, neither their lines of business nor their financial achievements are necessarily appropriate goals for any other company.

Corporate goals stated purely in financial terms do not provide much operational guidance for either the corporation with regard to the lines of business to engage in or for the divisions with regard to how to compete in the businesses they are already in. In this respect, they are not nearly as useful a guide to the formulation of strategy at either level as an accurate assessment of the strengths and weaknesses of the company and the opportunities these create in the environment.

Financial goals do affect the pressure felt within the organization to produce economic results on a current basis, and some such pressure is necessary in any economic organization. It is widely known that undue pressure for current performance can influence behavior in many ways, however, and that some of these can be to the detriment of the long-run health and reputation of the company. Indeed, one of the criticisms of diversified companies is that (intentionally or unintentionally) they apply undue pressure for profits to their divisions at times, resulting in a milking of divisions and a decline in the competitive position of companies that need not have occurred.

RISK

The degree of risk that a company management is willing to undertake in pursuit of profit, growth, or market position is an element of its strategy and becomes evident in the actions of the company. Historically companies tended to diversify when they had an excess of resources over what they felt they could profitably apply to their traditional businesses, even though those base businesses might not have been in trouble. When faced with trouble and declining prospects in the basic business, companies have often sought to reduce their overall risk by diversifying, with whatever resources they could spare, into areas that seemed more attractive. In the 1960s, however, a new category of risk taking appeared in which companies were very aggressive in obtaining resources for expansion in their pursuit of growth and were willing to subject themselves to both highly leveraged capital structures as well as unknown and possibly risky new businesses. The combination of highly leveraged financial structures, high-risk operating strategies, and the need to maintain a high price-earnings multiple on the stock in order to be able to continue making acquisitions on favorable terms resulted in a very high overall level of risk for some companies. Because of this high level of overall risk, setbacks that might otherwise not have been as important resulted in drastic declines in both earnings and stock prices of some of the more aggressive conglomerates in the 1969–72 period.

The conclusion to be drawn is not that one level of risk is preferable to others for all companies, but rather that the level chosen is up to management and is important. Some companies balance high business risk with conservative financing to arrive at an acceptable overall risk; many other combinations are possible. A low tolerance for risk may result in a rather uninteresting company and little chance of large gains. Strategies entailing a high level of risk are more likely to capture the imagination of both investors and managers, offering as they often do the prospect of large gains. Unfortunately such strategies may also lead to large losses, including possible loss of control of the company to creditors or acquirors. In any event, the attitude of management concerning the level of risk they feel comfortable with will affect many other aspects of the operations of the company, both at the corporate level and at the business-unit level.

RANGE OF DIVERSIFICATION

A difficult component of the concept of strategy at the corporate level of the diversified company is that which addresses the kinds of businesses the company will engage in and why. The allocation of funds to competing businesses presently within the corporation is an aspect of this problem, but it is much more amenable to analysis by means of various portfolio planning models that have been developed (and will be discussed later) than is the rationale for the product range of the company as a whole.

The range of product diversification can be viewed in primarily financial terms, such as profitability, growth, cash flow, degree of risk in the operations of the business that would affect the above, and so on. These measures can be applied to existing as well as potential businesses. In the case of possible acquisitions, the immediate impact of the acquisition on the earnings, earnings per share, and balance sheet of the acquiror are of great interest to managers and investors. Once some brave or naive soul has furnished estimates of future cash flows for the acquisition, computer programs are readily available to construct pro forma income statements and balance sheets to any degree of precision desired.

Although financial measures invariably need to be considered, they do not themselves constitute a sufficient basis for deciding upon the degree and type of diversification that should be pursued. If the anticipated influence of the acquiring company provides no reasonable basis for projecting different financial performance for a potential acquisition than would otherwise have occurred, then relying solely on financial measures to screen acquisitions would result in a product range comparable to the variety of companies represented in a nonspecialized common stock mutual fund. To confidently project different performance, a company must have a concept of its own strengths and the ways in which it can contribute to the operations of the acquisition and make use of what the acquisition might bring to the parent. This, in turn, requires a consideration of more than just financial criteria. If the nature of the business behind the financial statements is unimportant, the parent can more accurately be described as a holding company, not an operating or industrial company.

RELATED VERSUS UNRELATED DIVERSIFICATION

In considering diversification alternatives, it is natural to look first at those areas most closely related to the existing businesses. Indeed, management would be remiss not to do so since there is every reason to believe that familiarity is an advantage in evaluating and managing new opportunities and that it is easier to apply existing resources and skills to new opportunities if they are related in some manner. In addition, Rumelt's findings indicate that firms that engage in related diversification tend to have better performance than others, and those that engage in passive-unrelated have the worst records.

The way in which a particular acquisition or a diversification strategy can be justified in terms of research and development, manufacturing, marketing, or management skills that are related or complementary is important to examine and sometimes seems to be limited only by the ingenuity of those describing it. One type of relatedness can be viewed as what the corporation can contribute because of a general management ability that will be useful as an addition to, not a substitute for, the management of certain kinds of product divisions. Perhaps more frequently, relatedness is defined in terms of useful and more tangible skills in functional areas, an excess of physical resources, or technology that can be applied to an acquisition. In any event, the degree of relatedness of both present and prospective businesses is an element of the corporate strategy that you will want to examine.

It does not follow that a strategy of related diversification is preferable, however. Part of the difficulty stems from the problems of classification, especially for an outside observer. What is *related* in a meaningful sense, and what is not? The concept is surely more than a pair of boxes, one marked *related* and one marked *unrelated;* it is more like a continuum or a spectrum. In addition, new businesses can be related in some aspects—a common manufacturing process, for example, such as familiarity with precision plastic injection molding techniques—and totally unrelated in other important aspects of the business, such as the product design or marketing of plastic moldings for the aerospace as opposed to the toy business.

Relatedness is most commonly thought of as occurring with regard to knowledge or resources in the major functional areas such as research and development, manufacturing, and marketing, including the distribution system. It can also be important in the less tangible area of general management skills, which may be more relevent to some kinds of businesses than others. In assessing the importance of the degree of relatedness, you will have to judge both the degree of relatedness in specific areas as well as the importance of that area in the overall success of the business and the importance of the areas in which there are few or no related skills or resources.

A more serious problem than the one of classification exists for the manager who is attempting to apply the criterion of related versus unrelated to the choice of diversification strategies, however. As mentioned in Chapter 10, the profitability of expansion into any field depends partly on the skills and resources of the parent, partly on those of the acquisition, and partly on the extent to which each can contribute to the other. It also depends to a significant extent on the profitability of the field entered, however.

If the base industry is profitable, related fields are also likely to be so. This tends to be true especially for companies for which the base businesses have been profitable because of the existence of a significant core technology. General Electric and Eastman Kodak are good examples of companies with significant core technologies of this type. Part of the reason some companies which pursue a strategy of related diversification achieve superior performance, then, is that one of the conditions that make it attractive for a company to follow this strategy— an important core technology—is also associated with high performance.

Other types of barriers to entry, such as patents or distribution systems, may have similar effects. One needs to look to the base industry and company to determine whether the admitted risks of moving to less familiar territories outweigh the disadvantages of remaining close to the original business, continuing to apply skills and resources to related and familiar areas that may unfortunately have many of the very problems from which the company is trying to escape. The arguments favoring a strategy of related diversification are surely less applicable to a textile or cement company than to companies like Xerox or Polaroid, both of which have very substantial technical skills and (historically) extremely successful core businesses.

In spite of the difficulties we have with both classification and cause and effect as far as the related-unrelated dimension is concerned, it is important to think about present as well as future activities in terms of how they are, or can be, related to each other and to the distinctive competences of the company. The main benefits of doing so lie in four areas.

First, the degree of relatedness is some evidence of how good the judgment and knowledge of the parent is likely to be with regard to the requirements for success in the new industry and its ability to evaluate the positions and potential of the new acquisition. Indeed, the most important aspect of relatedness may be whether the parent has a strategic understanding of the needs of the new business which is insightful enough to enable it to see opportunities to improve the strategy or operations that others may have overlooked—not primarily whether one activity is related to another in a functional or market or technological sense.

Second, the more related the activities are, the more likely it is that the existing distinctive competencies of the corporate level will be useful. A corporate management that is thoroughly familiar with consumer packaged goods, for example, may have much to contribute to a venture in that field, even though there are no existing

divisions that could contribute people or products or specific resources to the new company. Similarly, basic technical knowledge
and experience in dealing with the problems of small, high-
technology companies may represent a highly useful resource, even
though there are no specific technical skills or facilities or patents
that are directly transferable.

Third, the more related the functional aspects of the possible
diversification effort are, the more likely it is that the functional
skills and resources of the parent will be of value to the acquisition.
If one activity is to make a contribution to the other, the skills or
resources have to be both applicable and available.

Finally, the more related the various businesses of the corporation are, the easier it is likely to be for the corporate level to understand the basic characteristics of each of their many businesses.
Understanding a company made up of divisions in real estate development, high-technology manufacturing, retailing, and insurance is
surely much more difficult than one with four divisions engaged in
manufacturing industrial products, even if the industrial products
are unrelated. In addition, whatever commonality exists will simplify the task of developing an appropriate role for the corporate
level with respect to the management of these businesses, an issue
which we shall discuss later.

It is important to look beyond the popular concept of synergy to
investigate just what the advantages will be that stem from relatedness. Perhaps the most important thing is to avoid the illusion of
relatedness, which has been used to justify almost any kind of diversification. One can get the impression from some of the announce-
ments accompanying acquisitions that the degree and importance of
the relatedness of an acquisition is limited only by the imagination
of the management. An extreme—but perhaps apocryphal—example
is that of the manufacturer of forklift trucks that was determined to
avoid falling prey to defining its business too narrowly. In its efforts
to avoid both marketing myopia and the limitations of its core business, the company decided it was really in the business of providing
vertical transportation and therefore diversified into escalators, with
disastrous results.

Although the related-unrelated dimension will not provide you
with an explicit guideline for selecting the best diversification strategy in the individual situation, it is a very useful way to begin investigating alternatives. We usually find it more comfortable to remain
with familiar activities. We have to remember that the very reason
companies diversify, however, is that the present activities no longer
meet the longer-term objectives. The more closely related the new
activities are to the existing operations, the greater the chance that
they will evidence similar problems. Carried to its logical extreme,

the most related diversification would represent no significant diversification at all, but merely an expansion of the existing activities.

SUMMARY

The concept of strategy as developed for the single-business firm requires some modification to be useful at the corporate level of the multi-business firm, but the essential elements remain. The detail on specific product-market strategies has to be much less, and the distinctive competencies of the corporation will have to be stated at a higher level of abstraction than for the single business. The establishment of long-term financial goals, risk levels, and type of product diversification all become more complicated as well. More attention will have to be paid to the fit of the corporate organization and its policies and strengths with the nature of the many businesses the corporation is in and the skills of operating management. Because of the complexity of the product lines, the large number of investment opportunities available, and the unavoidable distance of the corporate level from the actual operations of the businesses, however, the need for a clear corporate strategy is even greater for the diversified company than the for single-business company. We will turn to a framework of analysis for this purpose in the next chapter.

CHAPTER 13

A Framework
for Analysis

$\mathbf{T}$he purpose of these next three chapters is to describe an analytical approach to the corporate-level general management problems of diversified companies that builds upon the knowledge and skills you have developed in dealing with the job of the general manager in the single-business company. This chapter deals largely with the elements of the analytical framework introduced in Chapter 3 that deal primarily with the strategy formulation portion of the general manager's task. The subject of the next chapter is the allocation of financial resources in the diversified company, with considerable attention to the use of portfolio planning models in that process. The final chapter deals with the challenge of leadership at the corporate level in the diversified firm and the different roles of the corporate level that have evolved in both the formulation and implementation of corporate strategy in the diversified firm.

STRATEGY FORMULATION AND
IMPLEMENTATION OVER TIME

You will find that the discussion in these last chapters will, to a greater degree than most of the rest of this book, treat strategic and organizational issues together rather than separately. The division of the multi-business company, unlike the single-business company, has to deal with the organization structure imposed, the information and reward systems established, and the leadership style and abilities of a corporate level. The role the corporate level in the diversified company chooses to play in these matters and the effectiveness with which they are able to do so strongly affect the performance of the divisions and therefore of the overall corporation. Separating the process of strategy formulation from that of implementation is still useful for analytical purposes, but in dealing with the problems of corporate management in the diversified company, the distinction becomes even more difficult to maintain than for the single-business company.

You will also need to be concerned with the overall strategy and the approach to organization of the multi-business firm over time, and not just specific acquisition decisions or other large and visible resource allocations to a specific business. Such decisions are obviously important, and the larger the commitment in relation to the resources of the company, the more important they become.

The single acquisition or major resource allocation decision is to the corporate strategy of the diversified company, however, what the single capital expenditure project in a functional area is to the strategy of the single-business company. Both are important to do well, but both need to be part of a much broader overall strategy to make long-run success more likely. A strategy of making individual acquisition or investment decisions based largely on a financial analysis that does not take account of how the resulting business units will be managed, how they will relate to each other, and how they will contribute to the overall goals of the corporation is not any more likely to be successful than a capital-budgeting program in the single-business company that is unrelated to the strategy of the company. A series of financial decisions independently arrived at should not determine the strategy; the strategy should determine the financial opportunities investigated and pursued.

ANALYTICAL APPROACH

The most fruitful way for you to extend to diversified firms your understanding of the job of the general manager derived from your study of the single-business company is to build on the approach that you have already developed. To do so we will need to examine some of the ways in which the main elements of the analytical model portrayed in Chapters 3 and 8 need to be modified or thought of differently in order to make them useful for this purpose. We will also look in the next chapter at the application of portfolio planning models to the management problems of the diversified firm, as these can provide useful inputs to the analytical model.

The basic analytical model is most easily applied to the general management problems of the single-business firm. It suggests that the principal factors you should take account of in the process of formulating a corporate strategy are the environment of the company, the resources available or obtainable, the values of the management, and the broader responsibilities of the corporation. With regard to the implementation of strategy, the major factors you should consider are the organizational structure, the information systems, the reward systems, the allocation of resources, and your own leadership style and abilities. Finally, formulation and implementation, separable for intellectual purposes, need to be closely related in practice.

In applying that basic approach to the corporate-level general management problems of the diversified company, we will make use of the concepts already developed. We will also emphasize the importance of the concept of *fit* or *consistency* of the various elements of the model with each other in a manner suited to the problems and needs of the multi-business firm. In addition, we shall extend this same concept of fit to the relationships of the divisions with each other, with the corporate level, and with their individual external environments.

We shall also introduce a new concept, that of the *corporate role* in diversified companies. General management tasks are performed at multiple levels in the diversified company, and the role that the corporate level decides to play in the overall management of the corporation is important to each individual company. It is the means by which the corporate level can seek as well as maintain the most appropriate *fit* or pattern of relationships between the business units, the corporate level, and the external environment.

In continuing with the application of the analytical framework introduced in Part 2, we will turn next to the first of the major elements of that framework.

STRATEGY FORMULATION AND CORPORATE ENVIRONMENT

One of the consequences of diversification is that the strategic options of the firm are increased greatly, and the relevant environment can be as broad as the management wishes it to be. The general manager at the business level still has to be knowledgeable concerning his own environment, as described in Chapter 4. Managers at the corporate level, however, cannot possibly have as much knowledge about the environments of the many businesses in which they are engaged as the managers in the individual businesses can and should. Corporate staff units can of course be set up to become familiar with the various industries in which the company is engaged. When the number of different business units exceeds six or so, group officers can be used to ease the burden on the corporate president.

The degree to which different companies try to develop and maintain this expertise at the corporate level varies widely, as discussed further in Chapter 15.

Corporate officers in the diversified company nevertheless have to understand the industries in which they operate well enough to evaluate intelligently the performance of the managers of the businesses and take responsibility for the effective allocation of resources among the existing businesses and between the existing businesses and possible new businesses. The latter requires knowledge of a potentially unlimited number of outside industries or opportunities, and it is obvious that some means must be found to limit the sphere of interest and activity. That is the function of a corporate strategy, and especially that portion of it which defines what the distinctive competencies of the corporation are (or hopefully will be), thereby limiting the area of possible interest.

STRATEGY FORMULATION AND CORPORATE RESOURCES

In Chapter 5 we discussed the need to base the strategy for a company on a careful evaluation of the strengths and weaknesses of the company. Opportunities and aspirations may capture the imagination and even inspire action, but successful strategies need to take into account the distinctive strengths and unavoidable weaknesses of the company as well.

The need to explicitly consider just what the resources and distinctive strengths of the company are, or can be, is just as important in evaluating strategies at the corporate level of the diversified company as at the business level in the divisions. The corporate-level problem in the diversified company is more complex because the distinctive strengths, just as the strategy, generally have to be stated at a higher level of abstraction to be useful. It may be that a company wishes to define its basic competitive advantage in terms of a distinctive competence in supplying and selling mass-produced consumer packaged goods, for example, or working with high-technology firms, or specific kinds of technologies, or even strengths in the traditional functional areas. The challenge is not only to articulate such an approach in the annual report and to financial analysts, but also to develop and transmit within the firm the attitudes, skills, and resources required so that the result is a competitive advantage for the firm.

In the following sections we will discuss several major items relevant to an evaluation of the corporate resources of the diversified firm.

Financial Analysis

Just as with a single-business company, one of the first elements in your analysis should be to investigate the financial performance and position of the company. As explained in Chapter 5, among the measures important to look at are items such as the level and trend of sales, earnings, margins, return on equity, dividends, stock price and P/E ratio, as well as traditional balance sheet measures. You should be forewarned, however, that the diversified company is considerably more complex to analyze than the single-business company.

One reason is simply the result of the number of different businesses in which the firm is engaged. If four different businesses each are important with respect to their contribution to sales and earnings and use of assets, you will feel compelled to investigate the performance and prospects for each of them. If the company consists of 40 such units, you cannot investigate them all, but neither can you ignore them all on the basis that no one of them is very important. The usual solution to the problem of too many businesses to deal with is to consolidate them into fewer but larger units for analytical convenience. SBUs, product groups, and sectors, for example, serve this purpose. It should be apparent, however, that detail and understanding of the individual business is invariably sacrificed as the unit of analysis is broadened to include more and more businesses.

A second reason that your task is more difficult is that often the kind of information you would like to have is not broken out separately for public reporting purposes. The degree to which companies are required to report separately on their various lines of business, and how lines of business shall be defined, are matters of continuing discussion and negotiation between companies, accounting firms, the Securities and Exchange Commission, and other public agencies. There is considerably more information on business segments now than was available in the past, but for the larger and more diversified companies, the reporting breakdowns seldom get to the level of divisions. Few companies publicly disclose in their annual reports or 10-K statements more of a detailed breakdown of sales, profit, and assets employed than is required. For even our largest and most diversified companies, current requirements result in such figures seldom being shown for more than about six major reporting units. In 1982, for example, General Electric broke down their results into eight segments in their annual report, and Westinghouse only four.

If you then concentrate your attention on overall corporate figures rather than on product-market breakdowns, you will need to be careful that still a third difficulty does not lead you astray. For companies that have been engaged in acquisitions and divestitures, it is often difficult to ascertain just what portion of the performance can be attributed to internal growth and what portion was simply due to the arithmetic of the transactions. Financial data and the prices paid or received are not always reported publicly, and even if they were, to pull this data together can be a major task. In addition, both profit figures and balance sheet items are affected by the choice of accounting methods as well as by the terms of the transactions. Although the actual sources of the sales and earnings growth for companies engaged in acquisitions and divestitures can therefore be quite difficult to trace accurately, it nevertheless is important to make the best estimate possible as to the sources of performance for the diversified company.

None of this is intended to dissuade you from attempting a financial analysis of the diversified company as a part of your overall evaluation. If anything, this is more important to do carefully with the diversified company than with the single-business company. The performance and prospects of the single-business company are by definition the same as the performance and prospects of their existing operations. In any company which grows by acquisition, overall corporate results are the sum of the performance of the existing businesses as well as the financial consequences of the acquisitions (and divestitures) made each year. Separating these sources of performance to the extent possible is essential to an understanding of the diversified company.

To accomplish this, you will need to draw upon your knowledge of financial accounting and reporting practices, including how they have changed at times, to do the best job possible.[1] The difficulty of doing a careful job of financial analysis explains in part why financial analysts do not like dealing with highly diversified companies. Obtaining and analyzing the information necessary to truly understand the sources of their performance is considerably more burdensome than for a single-business company. The task of assessing the prospects of each of the many divisions in their various industries is an even more lengthy one and one which few outside analysts have the information, ability, or patience to do well.

General Management Skills

One important resource and therefore competitive advantage of the diversified company, claimed by many but difficult to verify, consists of the general management abilities of the group and corporate officers and staff. Such managers should be able to develop the organizational structures and processes so that their skills may be brought to bear in the individual situation on a continuing basis to provide both strategic and operational guidance to the many different business units of the company, thereby giving them an ongoing

advantage over their single-business competitors. Company statements and speeches by officials often include explicit statements as
well as unstated assumptions concerning the contribution of these
general management skills to the operations of the many divisions.
The effective exercise of such skills, made possible in part by the
formal control created by ownership, could provide a significant
distinctive competence for the diversified company.

The contribution made by such general management skills has
been much debated by both observers and members of diversified
companies, with little evidence developed concerning its value that
is convincing to those who hold opposing views. Most of us would
likely subscribe to the notion that there is a significant amount of
general business knowledge as well as a number of general management skills that can usefully be applied without long exposure on
the manager's part to each specific business that he deals with. The
success with which some managers are able to oversee or even become general managers of businesses they have little familiarity with
certainly provides support for that line of argument. Evidence of a
similar faith that there are general management skills that transcend
industry boundaries is the decision of most of the readers of this
book to invest their own time and money in trying to develop such
skills in an academic setting.

Strong arguments also can be made that the replacement of the
typical board of directors of the independent company with a knowledgeable and experienced group executive is likely to result in improved performance of the company as a division. The group vice
president, in addition to spending more time with the division on a
continuing basis than most directors are likely to do, also has the
advantage of broad experience, access to funds and additional experience and expertise from the corporate office, and the existence
of considerably more power to influence decisions, enforce more
planning, reward good performance, and penalize poor performance
than most outside directors or any outside consultant. The opportunity to exert such influence and provide such resources is a consequence of the formal structure of the diversified company. The
effectiveness with which it is done depends on the skills and knowledge of the managers involved, both corporate and divisional.

There are counterarguments as well, of course. These include
the disadvantages of imposing a superior over a division manager
who would likely much prefer to be his own boss, as would most of
us, and the bureaucratic effect of additional levels in the managerial
hierarchy, populated by executives who cannot be as familiar with
the many different businesses they are supervising as are the managers of the divisions. Managers of smaller divisions sometimes
complain that they are simply lost in the larger organization. In

recent years, there has been a considerable increase in the number of divisions sold to groups consisting of the division managements and outside investors in what are termed *leveraged buyouts*, where the hope is that the division will do better as an independent unit again with a highly motivated group of owner-investors than as part of a large organization.

Another important general management skill is shorter term in nature than the continuing influence discussed above. That is the ability to find companies which, as a result of whatever changes or additions the acquiring company seeks to accomplish in the relatively near future, can contribute significantly to the overall corporate purposes because of improved operations or freed resources. Obviously the more potential acquirors perceive that such contributions are possible, the higher the market price of the company will be as competitors bid up the price to reflect the value based on opportunities for the future, not just the record to date. The ideal situation would be one in which the potential acquiror sees great promise in a potential acquisition which others find uninspiring and therefore not worth much.

The ability to find such situations—and to be right—depends on the general management skills discussed previously. The changes can be of considerable variety. They can consist of such things as new strategies not contemplated, or at least not likely to be pursued, by the present owners or other potential acquirors; the pooling of resources or skills already existing within the corporation with the acquired company; and the more effective management of existing operations.

The contribution is not all one way, of course. An important factor in many acquisitions is how the new business can help the acquiring corporation (other than by providing immediate assets or earnings) without regard for what the new owner may be able to contribute to the operations of the acquisition. Examples of this kind of contribution could be additional marketing channels, needed manufacturing facilities or skills, patents, and so on. The most drastic short-term changes, of course, which often result in public criticism of the acquiring company, can consist of a debilitating transfer of cash resources back to headquarters, shutting down facilities, and even the partial or complete liquidation of the acquired company in order to free up financial assets.

As you have the opportunity to observe or read about the activities of corporate management in the diversified company, you should try to discern just what the contributions—and limits to the contributions—are of the group vice president or the corporate office to the operations of the divisions. All companies are interested in performing better than their competitors. The challenging task for you is to understand just how the various levels of management in the diversified company can contribute to this objective with regard to the operations of the divisions.

Management abilities and the accompanying strategy and organization structure that can take advantage of them to create superior operating performance on a continuing basis constitute an important corporate resource and distinctive competence, and they should result in a continuous process of true value creation. It is not an easy skill to develop or to replicate. This aspect of the management of diversified industrial companies is the most worthy of your efforts to understand and to master.

A word of caution is also in order, since seemingly unlimited faith on the part of some managements in their ability to improve the operations of the acquisitions they make has been necessary in order to justify the high premiums over market price paid in recent years for some acquisitions. Warren Buffet, an outstandingly successful money manager and chairman of Berkshire Hathaway, Inc., has made the following observations:

> Many managements apparently were overexposed in impressionable childhood years to the story in which the imprisoned handsome prince is released from a toad's body by a kiss from a beautiful princess. Consequently, they are certain their managerial kiss will do wonders for the profitability of Company T(arget).
>
> Such optimism is essential. Absent that rosy view, why else should the shareholders of Company A(cquisitor) want to own an interest in T at the 2X takeover cost rather than at the X market price they would pay if they made the direct purchases on their own?
>
> In other words, investors can always buy toads at the going price for toads. If investors instead bankroll princesses who wish to pay double for the right to kiss the toad, those kisses had better pack some real dynamite. We've observed many kisses but very few miracles. Nevertheless, many managerial princes remain serenely confident about the future potency of their kisses—even after their corporate backyards are knee-deep in unresponsive toads.[2]

Financial Resources and Skills

Financial resources are an important strength in any company. Excess funds are the most readily transferable resource of all. Such resources can come from many sources in a diversified company: a predictable operating cash flow in excess of current division needs, additional borrowing capacity, cash that could be freed up by better asset management or by the sale of some businesses, and so on. A projection of the sources and applications of funds available, a common financial analytical technique, is essential to an assessment of the opportunity (or limitation) provided by the financial resources of the company.

A major source of financial resources for the single-product companies that diversified around the turn of the century was cash generation from their existing businesses that exceeded their needs for reinvestment or dividend payments. An important (but temporary) financial resource in the development of some of the conglomerates more than a half century later was a reception in the capital markets that bestowed upon them a price/earnings ratio high enough to make the issuance of stock for new equity or as payment for the acquisition of other companies unusually attractive. Many of the conglomerates were able to obtain the financial resources necessary to support their rapid growth by acquisition in this manner.

The integrated petroleum industry in the late 1970s and early 1980s is a prime current example of an industry in which predictable large cash flows could provide resources for diversification on a scale far beyond that available to other industries and companies. The steel industry and the auto industry in the early 1980s are examples of just the opposite: industries suffering not from a cash surplus but a cash shortage. Just as existing or obtainable resources are an advantage, a shortage is a clear liability.

As you evaluate the diversification opportunities and plans of companies and industries, the financial resources available to support diversification strategy are essential to examine. A strategy of diversification which does not take into account the amount and source of the financial resources required is just as deficient as a strategy for a single business which identifies great opportunity but neglects to put a price tag on the effort and to identify the source of the funds.

It is not only the existence of financial resources that can constitute a strength, of course, but also the skill of the corporate management in allocating these resources to the existing businesses or to new businesses. This topic will be taken up in more detail in the next chapter, which deals with the context of the corporate financial allocation problem and the application of portfolio planning models to assist management in this process.

Finding Undervalued Situations

Some believe that the corporate level of the diversified company can develop a distinctive competence at finding and buying undervalued companies. These could be defined as companies that are available at a price that does not reflect their "true value" in terms of the returns likely to occur in relation to the risks present. The additional assumption is that these results can be obtained by treating the companies largely as passive investments, just like stocks held in a mutual fund, and therefore do not depend upon great management effort, brilliance, or any synergy resulting from the combination. The main skill is assumed to be that of identification and purchase of companies at a price that does not reflect their true market value. It is the modern-day version of the "buy low and sell high" recipe for success in the stock market, with the additional handicap that premiums of from 25 percent to 100 percent over the market price will almost surely have to be offered to gain control and ultimate ownership.

The results of numerous empirical studies indicate the improbability of any management being able to develop and exploit this skill on a consistent basis over a period of time, however. There is very little evidence that *any* particular investment strategy (other than with several qualifications to buy and hold a diversified portfolio of low P/E stocks) is superior, after adjustment for risk, to any other for the passive investor buying securities on the public market.[3] Certain strategies work well in specific markets but not in others, and there are few consistent winners in predicting what market conditions will prevail and therefore what strategies will be effective. There is no reason to believe companies should be better at this than individuals or financial institutions. Just as there are always examples of spectacularly successful stock market investments, there are also examples of specific acquisitions which did, in fact, turn out to be undervalued at the time. Such individual examples should not obscure the low probability that skills at picking winners exist with enough predictability to provide a competitive advantage over time for an operating company with regard to their diversification strategy.

Some companies have had an even shorter-run and more financially based strategy of accumulating an equity position in a target company, and possibly even making a formal unsolicited takeover offer, with the hope that the ensuing battles between the target and potential acquirers will enable the first company to sell out at a profit in a short time. This has been successful for some companies and individuals and does depend on distinctive strengths and skills for its success. It is far removed from the ongoing tasks of building and managing the diversified company, however, and will not be discussed further.

Resources and Skills: Conclusions

The purpose of this discussion of company resources and possible distinctive skills has not been to develop an exhaustive listing of these items. Instead, it is to suggest how the basic concept of corporate resources needs to be modified to make it useful at the corporate level of the diversified company. You will need to think carefully about each individual situation that you encounter to determine what the resources are that might be applied to new opportunities and what the distinctive strengths are that will enable the company to exploit its present opportunities most fully.

Diversified companies vary widely in the ways they perceive their corporate strengths and the ways in which they try to apply these strengths. Some, such as United Technologies under Harry Grey, seek a strong theme of central and advanced manufacturing technology with emphasis in the defense area. Others, such as Textron, believe their competence and contribution lie far more in the effective management of a wide variety of stand-alone manufacturing divisions which are in consumer, industrial, and defense markets. Litton originally placed great emphasis on the ability of the corporate level to recognize, manage, and combine technology of various types to create new approaches to commercial markets. Heublein, a very successful marketer of distilled spirits (and especially Smirnoff Vodka), acquired a large brewery and a large California winery largely because they believed the corporate marketing skills which had contributed so heavily to their success in distilled spirits would form the basis for success in the related businesses as well.

The challenge for the corporate level is to develop the distinctive strengths and acquire the resources needed to enable it to capitalize on the opportunities in the environment not just to uncover them or note that others have been able to exploit them successfully. If all a steel company management had to do was diversify into pharmaceuticals because that industry is more profitable and is likely to grow much more rapidly than the steel industry, low-margin steel companies or high-margin pharmaceutical companies would not exist for long. The fallacies in that line of thinking with regard to diversification strategy are in the presumptions that attractive companies are worth the high price that must be paid and that a troubled steel company can contribute to the operating performance of a pharmaceutical company.

In the diversified company, just as in the single-business company, successful results come not just from noting better opportunities elsewhere, but from the fit which follows from the creative and successful matching of opportunity with the competence to capitalize on it. Such a fit can only stem from a concept of your company's existing or attainable distinctive resources and skills that will enable you to take advantage of specific opportunities.

The point is not that certain definitions are inherently better than others, but rather that it is important to think through very carefully just what the rationale will be for choosing activities in which to engage and for managing those activities most effectively. As in all activities involving judgment, sometimes you win, and sometimes you lose. For Heublein, the United Vintners winery acquisition performed very well for many years, but the acquisition of Hamm's Brewery was a disaster. Hamm's was sold at a substantial loss after a decade of attempts to apply the marketing skills that had worked so well elsewhere failed to solve the structural problems of a large but second-level brewery competing in an industry where economies of scale were important in production as well as marketing and where industry consolidation had been a long-term trend.

In the absence of guidelines based on product, market, or technology characteristics, diversification is likely to stem largely from financial criteria, which can result in a very strange collection of businesses indeed. The financial logic which stems from purely financial guidelines and stock market opportunity can result in the creation of companies no industrial logic can justify.

STRATEGY FORMULATION AND MANAGEMENT VALUES

The concept of *management values* as it was developed in Chapter 6 needs little further elaboration or modification here. The impact of the top management on the rest of the organization is just as important in the diversified corporation as in the single-business corporation.

The major complicating factor with regard to management values is that more levels of management, with different perspectives and personal interests, have been added. Because of this, the division manager in the diversified company is not likely to have as much ability to impart his personal values on the goals or the behavior of his division as the president of the independent company does. The balance, as is the case with all of the areas of the general manager's responsibility and authority in the diversified company, evolves over time in each specific case.

STRATEGY FORMULATION AND CORPORATE RESPONSIBILITY

As far as corporate responsibility is concerned, several new issues arise because of the nature of the diversified corporation. Most of these fall under the general heading of the responsibility the corporation has and shows to local employees and communities.

Many claim divisions of multiunit companies are worse citizens of their local communities than are local companies because they are more likely to phase out marginal operations and consolidate even successful operations with other units elsewhere in the world, thereby reducing local employment. Defenders counter that even if the above is true, from a public policy point of view, society is better served by a shutdown or phasing out of the less promising operations in the portfolio of the parent's activities. The alternative of letting those businesses continue to struggle along with marginal results until bankruptcy overtakes them is seen as less kind to the individuals in the long run and less efficient for society with regard to the allocation of resources to their most efficient use. All agree that it is unfortunate that this must sometimes happen, as it usually involves high human costs for the people and communities affected.

Another area of criticism concerns the tendency of companies to move as many staff activities of an acquired company as possible back to the corporate headquarters and to reduce use of local outside professional services, such as legal and accounting help. One can argue, of course, that a consolidation or reduction of various staff and professional services is desirable if it results in lower overall costs to the company and therefore society, as is the intent. As with a reduction in employment resulting from production cutbacks, however, the benefits are distant, and the costs are local.

Critics also argue that the local manager of a division of a large conglomerate is likely to be less involved in community affairs, partly because he may be much more of a transient than the president of a local company would be and partly because the parent company is likely to be less concerned with the local community. Corporate contributions as well as executive time and interest are likely to suffer as a result.

Both states and local communities have often opposed the acquisition of local businesses by distant conglomerates, and a number of states have enacted antitakeover laws designed to make such acquisitions much more difficult. As a result of recent court cases, it appears that federal laws will override state laws restricting takeovers, and this avenue of local defense is likely to be ineffective.

At a broader level, the concentration of ownership of widespread and often seemingly disparate operating units that perhaps could be independent business units has frequently been questioned. Large and distant corporations are understandably viewed as more remote from local needs and control as well as more powerful in both economic and political matters because of their size. Unions often dislike diversified companies because of the decreased vulnerability of the corporation to the outcome of labor negotiations in any one division. Furthermore, it is difficult for any single union to seek to offset this advantage by gaining significant representation in a number of diverse and geographically distant operations. Even the U.S. Navy has found it more difficult to deal with shipyards that have been acquired by diversified companies since the shipyards then become stronger bargainers over defense contracts.

It is clear that the opportunity to diversify has been important to individual companies and that the pursuit of such opportunities has provided an important source of growth and stability for many of our industrial companies. Diversification has had a major effect on the structure of American industry, and it is likely to continue to do so in the future. There is a lack of clear empirical data as yet that such concentration results in improved economic performance for investors as a group or for society as a whole, however. The inconclusiveness of the aggregate empirical data eliminates one important counterargument to those would restrict such activity because of their concern about the concentrations of power which result from diversification by acquisition.

SUMMARY

Your approach to the problem of strategy formulation in the diversified company should be similar to the one you have developed for the single-business corporation. The task is more complex, as described in this chapter, but the same basic analytical framework can be extended to allow for the additional complications caused by large numbers of diverse businesses and the increased levels of management that are necessary as a result.

In the next chapter we will deal in more detail with the application of one common analytical tool, the portfolio planning model, to the resource allocation problem in the diversified company. The last chapter then focuses on the role of the corporate level in the management of the diversified company.

CHAPTER 14

Allocation of
Financial Resources

The diversified corporation cannot avoid playing a continuing role in the allocation of funds among the existing businesses and between the existing operations and possible new ventures. Influencing the allocation of resources so that they will flow to areas of greatest importance to the overall corporation is an important task of the corporate level in the diversified company. The skill with which this is done can constitute a significant competitive advantage if done well. In this chapter we will review briefly the nature of this challenge in the diversified company and describe logic underlying the application of portfolio planning models to assist management in this task.

CHALLENGE

In all companies the corporate level has the power to control the use of capital by the divisions, and few are the companies that do not exercise that power. Indeed, it is not possible to avoid influencing the spending by the divisions. Whether allocations of capital (or, more broadly, cash flow) and the consequent spending by the divisions are based on judgment, formula, or a combination of the two, the procedure chosen will have an effect on current division and corporate profits as well as on which business units spend resources for future growth and which units supply these resources.

Unfortunately there is no simple solution for the corporate level to the problem of determining the most appropriate profit goals and capital-spending plans of the various divisions. As described in

Chapter 11, there is no reason to believe that any single factor such as current profits, profit rates, market size or growth, capital project hurdle rates, or level of technology can indicate the areas of highest promise for the future and therefore most deserving of resources for strategic purposes. No matter what the formula chosen, some obvious weaknesses in the resulting allocations are likely to occur.

Companies spend much time and effort administering and trying to improve the corporate allocation process. The more diverse the company and the more numerous the units, the more difficult the task becomes and the more necessary it becomes to develop a more abstract framework or method of analysis to make up for the lack of firsthand knowledge of the divisions and industries themselves. The principal analytic method which has been developed in the last decade or so to deal with problems of this kind consists of the use of portfolio planning models, as described in the next section.

PORTFOLIO PLANNING MODELS

As we mentioned earlier, one of the significant advantages a diversified company has relative to the single-business company is the greater variety of opportunities to invest its financial resources. The diversified company can contribute to the cash needs of some divisions with the resources obtained from other divisions, whereas the single-business company must obtain any net cash inflow that its operations require by acquiring the funds—equity or debt—on whatever terms the capital markets will provide it. The diversified company has internalized the traditional capital market function with regard to the allocation of funds among its own businesses, and the invisible hand of the outside financial markets becomes the visible hand of the corporate management.

A strategy of shifting efforts or resources in the pursuit of increased returns or stability is neither new nor revolutionary; credit for the first attempts to do so must go to our ancestors who sought out more fertile gamelands, farming areas, or crops. Neither is the idea of using the resources of an older and established business to support the expansion of a more promising newer one within the same corporation. The accounts of early diversification moves of many of our major companies describe clearly the pattern of applying resources earned in existing businesses to more promising areas elsewhere.

Several developments have occurred in the last 15 years or so which provide considerable assistance to the manager in thinking about the nature of the resource allocation problem at the corporate level, however, as well as in providing guidelines for the actual allocations themselves. These developments consist of a basic conceptual scheme, a simple language system, and the collection of data that can lend empirical support to efforts to identify preferred mixes of businesses within the product portfolio and to the allocation of funds to those businesses on a continuing basis.

The basic concept you should be familiar with is the portfolio planning model, or PPM, as it has come to be called. The habit of thinking about the resource allocation problem in this manner is far more important than mastering the details of its application in the specific situation, as the latter requires considerable experience as well as more detailed market and cost information than companies themselves normally possess at the time they initiate such planning efforts.

Company Position and Industry Attractiveness

The basic purpose of a portfolio planning model is to combine measures of industry attractiveness with measures of a business unit's position in that industry to provide help to the manager who needs to make a judgment concerning the attractiveness of investment in that unit relative to other units. The widest popularization of this approach has been by the Boston Consulting Group. Their 2 × 2 matrix, as well as the logic of portfolio planning models, have been explained extensively in their own literature and elsewhere.[1] The essential elements of their matrix and the terms they have applied to the various quadrants are shown in Exhibit 14–1.

EXHIBIT 14–1
Market Share/Market Growth Matrix

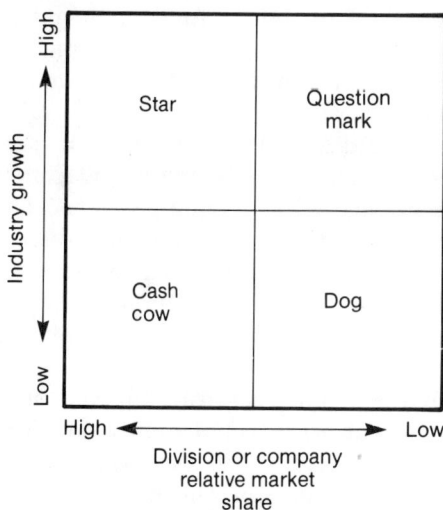

This matrix seeks to establish measures of relative industry attractiveness along the left-hand vertical scale and of the division's competitive position within the industry along the horizontal scale. In this simple format, the principal determinant of industry attractiveness is assumed to be the rate of growth of the industry. The relative market share of the particular company or division is considered the single most important variable in determining its position within the industry. Relative market share in this case is defined as share relative to the largest other competitor in the industry, with the middle vertical line usually assigned a value of 1.0.

The role of the matrix is to portray businesses in terms of their potential for generating cash flow. The nature of the business is not needed and is not shown on the matrix; it is presumed irrelevant to a consideration of the cash flow characteristics and opportunities that exist. If the growth rates of the industries and the relative market positions of two different businesses are identical, the businesses will appear to be identical on the matrix, even though one may be manufacturing wood stoves and the other integrated circuits.

With regard to the level of abstraction, then, this particular matrix is just as much removed from the details of the individual business as is the experience curve and the PIMS study of determinants of market profitability discussed in Chapter 5. They all seek to build models and derive hypotheses concerning the profit potential of businesses and business strategies that can apply to any business and that can therefore be used to compare businesses otherwise quite dissimilar. The advantages of being able to do so are great, especially when many diverse businesses must be considered. Indeed, the promise of freeing the corporate level from the time-consuming and difficult task of considering the substance of each of the many businesses competing for funds is the principal attraction of this form of analysis. The hazards of making judgments on the basis of such abstract data should also be apparent, however; simplicity always comes at a cost.

McKinsey & Co. and Arthur D. Little, Inc., both leading management consultants, employ similar graphic models to assist the manager in conceptualizing and analyzing problems. Their models are more detailed and qualitative in that they include more factors than just market growth and market share in arriving at judgments about industry attractiveness and company competence to succeed in that industry. An example of a more elaborate portfolio model is shown in Exhibit 14–2.

In this model, the factors that determine industry attractiveness are similar to and just as broad as those outlined in Chapter 4, which deals with strategy formulation and the corporate environment. The factors that determine the rank of a business with regard to its competitive strength are similar to those described in Chapter 5, which deals with strategy formulation and corporate resources. This more comprehensive model, then, incorporates an approach much more like the framework developed in this book than the simpler market growth versus market share model shown in Exhibit 14–1.

EXHIBIT 14–2
Industry Attractiveness Matrix

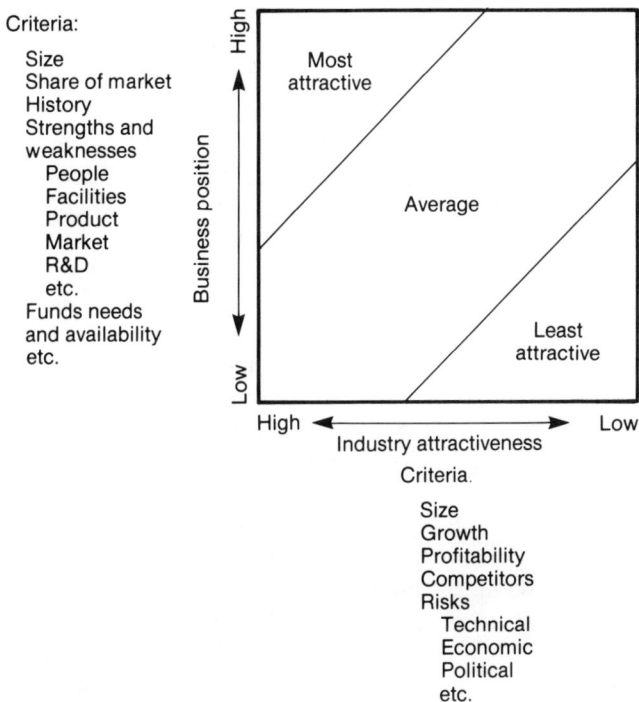

Criteria:

Size
Share of market
History
Strengths and
weaknesses
  People
  Facilities
  Product
  Market
  R&D
  etc.
Funds needs
and availability
etc.

Business position — High ↑ Low ↓

Most
attractive

Average

Least
attractive

High ← Industry attractiveness → Low

Criteria:

Size
Growth
Profitability
Competitors
Risks
  Technical
  Economic
  Political
  etc.

Many elaborations are made in the models, and their representation in graphic form is limited only by the ingenuity and budget of the graphic arts department. One refinement is to portray the various divisions of the company on the chart in terms of circles, with the area of the circles representing the relative size of the units in terms of sales, profits, or assets. Another is to construct such a chart for several points in time so that trends in the development of businesses can be observed. To assist the manager in predicting what countermoves important competitors are likely to make, charts can be prepared on competitors in order to assess what their options are and likely responses will be.

Cash Flow Patterns

The usefulness of this type of matrix is based on the assumptions that individual businesses can be reliably located within the matrix based on the criteria used, that specific patterns of cash flows are associated with each of the various quadrants, and that the primary measure of the attractiveness of a business is the pattern of cash flows over time. For example, a division with a dominant position in a high-growth industry (a "star") will probably require an inflow of cash in its early stages in order to maintain its position during the period of high industry growth. It is of course possible that such a company will be profitable enough to finance its high growth from internal resources, but that is unlikely if there are other strong competitors for market leadership. The attractiveness of the star is that the net cash inflow likely to result from the position of market leadership as the growth slows down and profit levels increase will far outweigh the earlier investment in gaining and keeping market share.

As the growth rate begins to decline in an industry which was growing rapidly, the business which was dominant in this industry drifts into the "cash cow" category. Such businesses are highly useful in providing the cash needed to finance the stars when they need it. They are also essential in supporting the "question marks" as well—those companies for which the future is promising because of the high industry growth projections but uncertain because of the low relative market share position of the specific division.

Companies with a small market share in slowly growing industries are considered to be "cash traps" or "dogs," where the potential gain is unlikely to merit the investment of cash, management effort, and time required to eventually bring the business into a more promising quadrant. The usual prescription is that divisions in this category should be sold, as they do not even have the promise of success that exists for the question marks.

Portfolio planning models are designed to help the manager construct and maintain a portfolio of businesses which is balanced in the sense that there are sufficient cash cows to provide the cash flow to support the question marks and possibly the stars, if they need it, and to ensure the continued emergence of stars as companies and industries decline and become less attractive for all participants over time. If this can be accomplished, it will contribute to the continued growth and renewal of the company as well as avoid the need for external financing, results much prized by most managements.

Application

A great deal has been written about the logic, the application, and the usefulness of various analytical planning models. A very useful discussion of the use, evolution, and impact of portfolio planning models in the large diversified company, based on detailed clinical research as well as on survey data from a sample of several hundred companies drawn from the Fortune 1,000, is contained in an article by Haspeslagh.[2] He emphasizes the importance and difficulty of focusing on the strategic missions of carefully defined SBUs in their actual marketplaces and avoiding labels and simple rules of competition, of integrating the allocations that result with the business plan, and of investing corporate management time in the review process. He describes several stages in the evolution of the use of portfolio planning models in the diversified company and estimates that "only 14 percent of the Fortune 1,000 have reached the most advanced stage," a process which seems to take at least five years.

An important assumption of portfolio planning models is that the businesses plotted can be considered as separate units for the purposes of such analysis. In practice, this makes the consideration of any interdependencies among divisions or SBUs difficult to handle. It may also require the specification of business units for strategic planning purposes that differ from present organizational structure and reporting relationships and which therefore also are likely to be different than established patterns of accounting data, historical information, profit responsibility, and line authority. Such conflicts obviously contribute to the difficulty of integrating the portfolio planning process with the administrative structure and practices of the company.

The concept of strategic business units or SBUs came into use largely because of the need for a way to describe businesses or groups of businesses in ways that are useful for portfolio planning purposes at the corporate level. Companies that have seriously pursued portfolio planning methods have first had to carefully group their businesses into SBUs and then collect market and cost data to fit these new definitions. As both Haspeslagh[2] and Hall[3] have pointed out, this is both important and difficult. Interestingly enough, Haspeslagh found that the number of SBUs considered at the corporate level seldom exceed about 30, even in large and diverse companies with a far greater number of divisions and profit centers. It appears that if the number of units to be considered at the top level becomes too large, the task once again becomes unmanageable even with the assistance of these more abstract analytical approaches, and the data are aggregated further in order to be more useful.

It should also be apparent that the same cautions and reservations that apply to the application of experience curve data and PIMS analyses for the individual business apply to the application of a product portfolio approach built on these concepts. An article by Woo and Cooper,[4] which identifies 40 successful low market share businesses, and an article by Hamermesh,[5] which describes successful strategies for low market share businesses, each constitute a reminder that, as pointed out in Chapter 4, there are numerous exceptions to the guidelines provided by such analytical aids.

In addition, unforeseen and uncontrollable external changes can have major strategic impacts, both positive and negative. The classification system does not have the validity of Newton's Laws of Motion. Classifying a division as a star does not necessarily mean that it now is or ever will be one. Mistakenly classifying a company as a dog may to a substantial degree be a self-fulfilling prophecy, however, with unfortunate consequences to all. And forcing a company to be a generator of cash is very likely to have an adverse effect on its ability to grow, a situation that may be desirable at times from the corporate point of view but one that can easily have unintended adverse consequences.

Finally, a very substantial management problem that the portfolio planning models do not address, and which the facile terminology does little to ease, is that of the administrative difficulties of implementing whatever allocation decisions are made. It is all well and good to decide as a result of portfolio analysis that a given division is a dog, but how would you like to be the division manager of an operation so categorized? How would you explain the corporation's view of your division to your management team, understandably concerned with their own careers? How would you explain the career opportunities to graduates you would like to hire? And how would you feel as a new employee if you had not been informed about the dim view of the future that the corporation held about the division in which you were beginning your career?

It is for such reasons that companies are often not as explicit in the communication of their decisions, and the reasons for them, as the analytical framework would permit them to be. Even without labels or reasons, the resulting allocations can cause unproductive anxiety and opposition, which require both skill and tact to overcome. Publicly identifying winners and losers has high costs, and companies look for ways to make the judgments and resulting allocations less threatening to everyone.

SUMMARY

Portfolio planning models represent a way to estimate what the cash flows into or out of divisions will be under various assumptions. A portfolio model is also useful in helping to identify the cash flow characteristics of businesses that are being considered as additions to the product portfolio. This does not differ conceptually from a principal objective of strategic planning for the single-business company, which is also to provide a means for estimating potential cash flows under a variety of possible strategies.

A number of limitations in the usefulness of portfolio planning models have been noted. It should be evident that there are few if any rules or techniques that can be applied with success in a mechanical way to as complex a situation as the competitive business environment. The usefulness of the portfolio model for the diversified company, however, is that it does facilitate the comparison of many alternatives under complex circumstances. It also makes more evident the advantages of moving resources from one activity to another, as well as the need to have a portfolio in which the sources and uses of cash are at least in rough balance. For the corporation as a whole, simple arithmetic indicates that cash needs which cannot be met from the divisions themselves can only come from corporate resources or external capital markets.

The data necessary to do a thorough job of applying a portfolio planning model to the problems of a specific company are seldom found either in the public domain or in business school cases designed for classroom use. Indeed, defining and gathering the relevant data is one of the major tasks in constructing a portfolio planning model for an actual company. As you analyze the strategic position and options of a diversified company, however, it is more important to keep in mind the concepts underlying the portfolio planning model, to use whatever data are available to you, and to make assumptions where necessary. Questions of the relative promise of the various businesses and the cash they can either provide or will require are important factors for all diversified companies to consider.

CHAPTER 15

Corporate Role and Leadership

In this final chapter we will address the important issue of the corporate role in the formulation and implementation of strategy in the diversified company. We have said much in the previous chapters about the evolution of the diversified company, the complexity of the management tasks caused by the product diversity, and an analytical approach that is useful to general managers in such companies. We have said relatively little about the various ways in which the corporate level can fulfill its leadership role in the management of the overall corporation.

For the diversified company, a major element of the corporate strategy is what the role of the corporate office will be in contributing to the operations of the divisions and to the overall performance of the corporation. That role should be influenced strongly by a vision of what the distinctive competence of the corporation as a whole is or can be, and not just the strengths of individual divisions. It affects the formulation of strategy at the corporate and division levels as well as the organization structure and processes by which the strategies—corporate and divisional—are implemented. Even more so than in the single-business company, corporate strategy and the approach to the implementation of that strategy via organization structure and management processes are highly interdependent and are influenced by the role that the corporate office chooses to define for itself. The role chosen both stems from and helps define the overall strategy or business mission of the corporation.

The role of the corporate level in developing and maintaining such a distinctive competence can take many forms. It can consist of acquiring and managing in a highly decentralized way traditional and relatively large-sized manufacturing businesses, as in the case of Textron. It can consist of a much stronger management role and larger corporate staff actively overseeing a much broader range of businesses, most of them acquisitions, as in the case of IT&T. It can consist of even more management involvement in businesses originally related to each other by a technological base, as in the case of General Electric and Westinghouse.

The issue of what role the corporate or group levels should play in division matters is one of continuing concern to diversified companies, and one that is especially evident in times of crisis or stress. The problem is not just what the best solution is to a specific issue of a division investment or strategy or pricing or interdivisional conflict, but rather who decides what the best solution is, using what criteria, and how such problems should be decided on a continuing basis.

TWO BASIC APPROACHES

The degree of involvement of the corporate level in the affairs of the divisions can be thought of in terms of a spectrum, with "laissez-faire" or "hands-off" at one end and "managed" at the other:

"Laissez-faire"	"Managed"
<— —————————————————————————————————————	———————————————————————————— —>
Conglomerates	Diversified Industrials
Small headquarters staff	Large headquarters staff

Companies commonly referred to as conglomerates tend to be at the left end of this spectrum. Such companies tend to have diversified primarily by acquisition, often of seemingly unrelated activities, and usually within the past 25 years or so. Textron, Gulf + Western, Walter Kidde, and Litton Industries are well-known examples of this type of company. Companies that tend to fall into the right-hand category of "managed" are more likely to be the older industrial companies whose acquisitions took place long ago, if at all, and which have diversified primarily through building upon existing and often technically based skills into related areas. General Electric, Westinghouse, Koppers, and Ingersoll-Rand are examples of this category of diversified industrials.

It is clear that ways of managing the divisions and the approach to tasks and staffing at the corporate level are often associated with the history of diversification. Conglomerates tend to have much smaller corporate staffs in all areas than do the older diversified companies. The disparity is especially true with regard to functions such as research and development, marketing, and production. These frequently are not present at all at the corporate level in conglomerates but are commonly present in the diversified industrials. Field research in 10 Fortune 500 companies in 1970 demonstrated the prevalence of these two different approaches to the management of diversity by the two different types of companies, and subsequent research in the same companies in 1982 has confirmed their continued existence.[1] These two extremes represent fundamentally different conceptions of the role of the corporate level in the management of diversity and the distinctive competence it wishes to develop and exploit.

These two categories are presented not because all companies fall into one category or the other or even must remain where they presently are. Examples of companies can be found over the entire spectrum, with the majority somewhere in the middle. Just as the choice of leadership style and behavior—as described in Chapter 9—is of concern to the general manager of the single business, the role of the corporate level in the diversified company is a recurring question for many companies, however. The visible shortcomings of any present approach and the hoped-for advantages of an alternative approach often result in movement along the spectrum, as companies seek the balance best for them. If you become engaged in either line or staff activities at the division or corporate levels in a diversified company, you will soon become aware of the prevalence of these kinds of issues and the importance to the individuals of the way in which they are resolved.

PRESSURES FOR CENTRALIZATION

It is not too difficult to draw up a list of functions that can be performed both more cheaply and with greater expertise at the corporate level than at the division level. Activities such as dealings with the SEC, external financial relations of all kinds, compliance with and reporting on government regulations broadly affecting the conduct of business, and many legal matters, for example, are generally performed at the corporate level. When it comes to matters more closely related to the strategy and operations of the divisions, such as research and development, manufacturing, and marketing, however, the arguments in favor of centralization become much more complicated, and the approaches diverge more.

Of course, there is always the temptation to want to become involved in all the important decisions made in the divisions in the interests of improving the quality of the decisions. If there is much commonality in the manufacturing or marketing activities of the various divisions, even though they may be in completely separate businesses, both the temptation and the ability to become more involved increase. There are also numerous opportunities to encourage, if not require, interdivisional cooperation in matters that the divisions themselves might not pursue of their own free will. Purchasing of common items can be centralized, transportation fleets coordinated, use of other divisions to supply components formerly bought from outside suppliers encouraged, and so on. And in any decentralized organization, there will always be questions as to whether decisions made by the divisions are also in the best interests of the corporation. Finally, whenever a crisis occurs in a division, the reaction of the higher levels is most often to get more involved, even if their lack of involvement is not what caused the trouble in the first place. The crisis that might have been avoided or the sharp-pencil economies that can be achieved by coordinating purchasing, transportation, computer services, or dozens of other activities are easy to demonstrate. The adverse effects of more central staff and direction on the initiative, flexibility, and accountability of the divisions are much more intangible and subject to judgment and debate.

Even the most casual observation of organizations indicates that pressures such as these to centralize decision making are common. Decision making takes time, however, and top managers are under severe time pressures. A natural solution to these time pressures is to create more staff at the corporate level. The staff can then take the time that the line managers are unable to spare to become as familiar with the divisions as necessary. The staff can brief the manager, analyze and recommend action to him, or act in his stead.

The dilemma of the corporate level in the role it chooses to play with regard to the innumerable decisions and issues in which it could become involved is similar to that of the general manager of the single-business company in his dealings with his functional subordinates. Both have to decide how much they wish to, and are able to, become involved in the affairs of their subordinates. The more the corporate level in the diversified company wishes to become involved in the substance of decisions in the divisions, the more information they will need if they are not to act capriciously. As more information is gathered, however, the more the temptation is to assemble staff to check, analyze, and interpret it for the corporate manager. More people then are also needed at the division level, not only to assemble the reports, but to deal with the questions of the corporate staff so that the division manager can remain free to spend his time on the demanding job of running the division. Before long there will be staffs talking largely to staffs, hardly a happy outcome.

But if the parent has little staff and scanty information at the corporate level, the company is little more than a financial holding company, hardly a happy outcome either.

For general managers at the corporate level to routinely immerse themselves deeply in the affairs of any single division, either directly or vicariously through the mechanism of a staff, is no permanent solution to the problem. There **is** a general manager in the division. The reason the product division form of organization developed was to **separate** the management of the product division from the management of the overall corporation, not to combine them. No corporation will permit its divisions to be completely independent of any corporate involvement and influence; but at the same time most corporations want to create the best possible motivational climate for the managers in the divisons. What the corporate level sees as proper involvement and efficient administration may very well be described by division management as bureaucracy and interference. Conflicts are inevitable.

Your challenge is not to settle upon one approach as better than all others for all situations, but to try to think through what the most useful role of the corporate office is in the particular situation. An essential element of the strategy of some diversified companies is a concept of what a professional and powerful corporate staff with specialized skills can do to contribute to the operations of the divisions. Others, as described earlier, have very different ideas as to the most useful role for the corporate office. Many companies have gone through the process of building up their corporate staff, only to deemphasize the activity after a few years because it did not work as well as had been expected. The choices made are partly a matter of style or personal preference; but much also depends upon the kinds of businesses the corporation is in, the strategies adopted for competing in them, the skills of the division and corporate management, and the approach that has evolved over time.

IMPLEMENTATION AND LEADERSHIP

The general manager in the diversified company can influence the organization by means of the same variables as the manager of the single-business company. As described in Chapter 8, the organization structure, the information systems, the policies on measurement and reward of managers, the allocation of resources, and the intangible but vitally important matter of personal leadership are all important in leading and guiding any organization in the accomplishment of its strategic goals.

The appropriate mix of these influences available to the general manager is more complex but not different in kind in the diversified company. Just as with simpler companies, you will want to concentrate on what is most appropriate for the given situation. Organization structures inevitably reflect a compromise between the desire to have as few levels of management as possible in the chain of command while still not permitting the number of units reporting to any one individual to exceed six or so. Information systems need to balance the amount and type of information given to higher levels not only with the cost of assembling it but with questions of whose responsibility it should be to monitor and take action on such information, on what matters various levels of management should be spending their time, and how much information higher levels of management need and can assimilate. It is quite possible to provide the chairman of General Electric with a video console on which he can call up the number of toasters sold in Seattle the day before, for example. It does not follow, however, that looking at such information is a good use of the chairman's time nor a useful influence on the eight or so levels of management between the chairman and the salesman who sold the toasters.

With regard to the system of incentives and rewards, it is clear that the greater the degree to which individual incentives reward performance that clearly is in the corporate benefit, the less the amount of involvement required by the corporate level to ensure that decisions made throughout the corporation are in the corporate interest and not just the subunit or the individual manager's self-interest. The opportunity for firsthand observation of managers by the corporate president decreases as the company grows and diversifies, however, and this often results in placing more reliance on formal performance measures. The problem, of course, is that it is difficult to structure reward systems so that little oversight is needed, and the more such systems attempt to be congruent with the corporate interests in all respects, the more cumbersome and detailed they become. Once again it is a trade-off. The balance appropriate to the businesses and the culture of the company is to be sought, and not the one right answer.

The role of the manager as the leader of the organization, as described in Chapter 9, is just as important in the diversified company and even more difficult, in spite of the large number of other general managers attending to various portions of the business and the existence of specialists and established procedures to deal with many ongoing tasks. Although the president of the $10 million single-business company and the president of the multibillion-dollar diversified company are both general managers and leaders of their own organizations, the intellectual and emotional challenges are quite different. But such differences exist in many fields of organized endeavor—the challenges facing the 2d lieutenant and the general or the priest and the archbishop also differ greatly from each other. All are leaders, however, all have an important influence on their organizations, and all need to adapt their roles as leaders to their own abilities and the requirements of the situation.

SUMMARY

As you continue to develop your knowledge about and skills in dealing with the general management problems of all kinds of companies, both diversified and single-business, you will not have the benefit of a rigorous or comprehensive general theory. You will have to rely on the application of a basic but imprecise general approach such as the one we have developed, plus a generous application of common sense, judgment, and whatever experience you can bring to bear. Fortunately, these are attributes which companies reward far more handsomely than knowledge of theories and concepts useful in the classroom but limited in their application to practice.

As you decide for yourself what role you will play as a general manager or what kind of advice you will offer with regard to the problems we have been discussing, it is important to keep in mind that the way any one problem can be solved is not necessarily the way such problems can or should be solved on a continuing basis. Acceptance of this fact is difficult for many, but it is essential to an understanding of the true problems of general management and particularly those of managing diversity. Operating managers even in the single-business company who have succeeded primarily by immersing themselves in the substance of specific problems will increasingly be at a handicap as they rise to general management positions if they are unable to adjust, both intellectually and emotionally, to the increasing need for delegation and detachment. It is also difficult for students and scholars, accustomed to applying a solution worked out for a specific problem to a general category of similar problems, to accept that such an approach often breaks down in the administrative reality and complexity of the general manager's job, particularly in the large, diversified corporation.

Your concern should always be with the degree to which the main elements of the analytical framework described are supportive of and consistent with each other. No strategies, organizational approaches, or leadership styles are "best" in isolation of each other, of your skills and interests as a general manager, or of the situation in which they must be applied. Your challenge is to find the creative fit among these elements that best reconciles the goals management is seeking, the opportunities in the environment, and the administrative history and the resources of the company. These goals, resources, opportunities, and strategies will differ for companies, just as they do for each of us in our own lives.

In this book we have presented a general approach to managerial problem solving that you can apply to the specific situations you are likely to encounter. We have not tried to give you a handbook of correctly solved problems or a set of principles or checklists, because we believe these would be of less value to you in practice. Our objective has been to help you develop your own skills at analyzing the problems of the general manager, advising him on courses of action, and ultimately acting effectively yourself in that important, challenging, and rewarding role.

Supplementary Readings

The number of readings that are relevant to the practice of management is large. Books by practitioners and academics, articles from a variety of academic journals and business publications, and current newspaper stories all compete for our attention. Just as in a listing of the best restaurants, it is inevitable that someone's favorite will be omitted.

In this appendix we will list a number of books that we have found useful to recommend to those interested in the practice of management. It is not a "recommended reading list" in the sense that anyone should read all of the books on the list. On the other hand, all could benefit from reading at least a few of the books, if only to gain an impression of how the viewpoints and opinions of those who have studied certain aspects of management can be of help to you. Because most of the books contain extensive bibliographies and references, the list should also provide you with a starting point for reading more about any specific topic in which you are interested.

We have made no attempt to list articles. The largest single source of practitioner-oriented articles is the *Harvard Business Review*, and there is a Reprint Series that consists of about 15 HBR articles on related subjects bound together in books. At present there are 29 books of such reprints dealing with general management and 120 books in total; a series catalog listing the contents of each book is available from the *Harvard Business Review*, as listed in the bibliography. Individual reprints are also available.

Other academic journals that contain articles dealing with management include *The Sloan Management Review, The California*

Management Review, Business Horizons, The Columbia Journal of World Business, The Journal of Business Strategy, and *The Strategic Management Journal.* The most useful business periodicals include *Business Week, Fortune, Forbes,* and *Barron's.* By far the most influential and widely read business newspaper is *The Wall Street Journal;* anyone interested in current business events should at least skim it frequently. *The New York Times* also has an excellent but much shorter business section.

Quite apart from business-oriented materials, there is a world of literature relevant to the study of policy formulation and administration in governmental, church, and military as well as business organizations. Biographies and autobiographies offer other rich accounts of policy formulation and decision making. Similarly, history and political science provide opportunities to study the evolution of policy and organization in a more disciplined way. Accounts as diverse as those on the administrative organization set up in France by Napoleon in the 18th century, the development of the railroads in the 19th century, and the path of the social revolutions in the 20th century all offer clues about how leaders of organizations act effectively. Your problem will be to select a manageable number of items to read, and to develop the ability to select and use readings wisely.

In order to assist you in finding the books that may suit your particular interests and needs, we have noted the principal emphasis of the books in terms of five rough categories: general (G), formulation of strategy (F), implementation of strategy and leadership (I), diversification (D), and other (O). The categories are certainly not precise, and many books fall into several categories. The categories, however, along with the brief comments about the books, should provide you with some guidance beyond the title as to what the books are about.

READINGS

Emphasis

G   Andrews, Kenneth R. *The Concept of Corporate Strategy.* Rev. ed. Homewood, Ill.: Dow Jones-Irwin, 1980.

An excellent overview of and conceptual approach to general management organized around the concept of strategy.

F,D   Ansoff, H. Igor. *Corporate Strategy: An Analytic Approach to Business Policy for Growth and Expansion.* New York: McGraw-Hill, 1965.

Relatively simple and straightforward explanation of strategic alternatives with emphasis on diversification decisions.

Emphasis

G   Barnard, Chester I. *The Functions of the Executive.* 30th Anniversary Edition. Cambridge, Mass.: Harvard University Press, 1968.

The classic in the field, generally at a high level of abstraction, and like Adam Smith, not easy reading. First published in 1938, it has outlasted thousands of competitors.

D   Biggadike, E. Ralph. *Corporate Diversification: Entry, Strategy and Performance.* Boston: Division of Research, Harvard Business School, 1979.

A well-researched study of the time period (about seven years) and difficulties of bringing internal new ventures to a profitable level.

I   Bower, Joseph L. *Managing the Resource Allocation Process.* Homewood, Ill.: Richard D. Irwin, 1973.

A clinically based detailed description of the administrative realities of the capital budgeting process in a large, complex company.

O   Carr, Edward H. *What Is History?* New York: Alfred A. Knopf, 1961.

Nothing to do directly with business, but excellent as a reminder that authors and researchers often find what they are looking for—a caution to discern "what kind of bees are in his bonnet" as you evaluate any author.

G,D   Chandler, Alfred D., Jr. *Strategy and Structure: Chapters in the History of Industrial Enterprise.* Cambridge, Mass.: MIT Press, 1962.

A much-quoted classic by management researchers, the book shows how corporate strategies of diversification influenced organizational structures in large corporations. The introductory and concluding chapters provide an excellent overview.

G   Chandler, Alfred D., Jr. *The Visible Hand.* Cambridge, Mass.: Harvard University Press, 1977.

Historical account of the development of professional (as opposed to owner/founder) management in the American corporation. A Pulitzer Prize winner.

G,I   Cyert, R. M., and J. G. March. *A Behavioral Theory of the Firm.* Englewood Cliffs, N.J.: Prentice-Hall, 1963.

A skillful attempt to integrate theory with practice by describing the observed behavior of firms in terms of the self-interests of the individuals within it.

Emphasis

G   Drucker, Peter F. *The Practice of Management.* New York: Harper & Row, 1954.

An early, simple, highly readable, and eminently worthwhile book on management.

G   Drucker, Peter F. *Management: Tasks, Responsibilities, and Practices.* New York: Harper & Row, 1974.

An enormous compendium of opinion and observation on virtually every aspect of management from one of the most widely read and quoted business writers.

I   Gardner, John W. *Self-Renewal.* New York: Harper & Row, 1963.

An excellent short and readable book on the problems of maintaining vitality in both organizations and people.

G   *HBR Reprint Series.* Boston: Harvard Business Review, various dates.

A series of books containing reprints of Harvard Business Review articles on related subjects. At present there are 29 books on general management alone; an index is available from the HBR.

O   Helfert, Erich. *Techniques of Financial Analysis.* 5th ed. Homewood, Ill.: Richard D. Irwin, 1982.

Highly explicit, straightforward book on techniques of financial analysis for the practitioner.

I   Kotter, John P. *The General Managers.* New York: Free Press, 1982.

A detailed description of how general managers actually spend their time.

G   Lawrence, P., and J. Lorsch. *Organization and Environment.* Boston: Division of Research, Harvard Business School, 1967.

An exploration of the nature of and need for a fit between the organization and its environment.

F   Lorange, Peter. *Corporate Planning: An Executive Viewpoint.* Englewood Cliffs, N.J.: Prentice-Hall, 1980.

An extensive description of long-range planning problems and approaches in the large company.

D   Mace, Myles, and George Montgomery, Jr. *Management Problems of Corporate Acquisitions.* Boston: Division of Research, Harvard Business School, 1962.

An old but still highly relevant book on the management problems of acquisitions, based on personal experience and extensive field of research.

Emphasis

G   Mintzberg, Henry. *The Nature of Managerial Work.* New York: Harper & Row, 1973.

        A thorough exploration of what managers do, in conceptual terms, based on observation of practice.

G   Peters, Thomas, and Robert Waterman. *In Search of Excellence.* New York: Harper & Row, 1982.

        An attempt to generalize about the management characteristics and practices that contribute to successful performance. A smashing best seller in 1983.

F   Porter, Michael E. *Competitive Strategy.* New York: Free Press, 1980.

        A highly structured approach to the analysis of industries and competition which draws considerably on findings from industrial organization—a field of economics.

G   Quinn, James B. *Strategies for Change.* Homewood, Ill.: Richard D. Irwin, 1980.

        A careful and persuasive analysis of how managers in fact do plan, which is far more incremental in nature than commonly thought.

D   Rumelt, Richard P. *Strategy, Structure, and Economic Performance.* Boston: Division of Research, Harvard Business School, 1974.

        A carefully researched book on the relationships between strategy, structure, and performance based on an analysis of over half of the Fortune 500 companies.

D   Salter, Malcolm S., and Wolf A. Weinhold. *Diversification Through Acquisition.* New York: Free Press, 1979.

        A comprehensive exposition of the history and logics of diversification via acquisition.

D   Schendel, Dan E., and Charles W. Hofer, eds. *Strategic Management: A New View of Business Policy and Planning.* Boston: Little, Brown, 1979.

        A detailed development of an approach to strategic management with extensive reference to research concepts and findings.

I   Selznik, Philip. *Leadership in Administration.* Evanston, Ill.: Row, Peterson, 1957.

        A short classic on the importance of creating values that can be "institutionalized" by the organization, as well as creating and maintaining a "distinctive competence."

Emphasis

G   Sloan, Alfred P., Jr. *My Years with General Motors.* Edited by John McDonald and Catharine Stevens. Garden City, N.Y.: Doubleday Publishing, 1964.

A highly readable and informative account of the development of General Motors and the managerial concepts necessary to manage it.

F   Steiner, George. *Strategic Planning.* New York: Free Press, 1979.

A thorough account of strategic planning problems and practices.

D   Vancil, Richard F. *Decentralization: Managerial Ambiguity by Design.* Homewood, Ill.: Richard D. Irwin, 1979.

A research-based exposition of the problems of and various solutions to the need to decentralize authority in the diversified corporation.

F   Warren, Kirby. *Long Range Planning: The Executive Viewpoint.* Englewood Cliffs, N.J.: Prentice-Hall, 1966.

A short, readable, practitioner-oriented discussion of long-range planning.

I   Zaleznik, Abraham. *The Human Dilemma of Leadership.* New York: Harper & Row, 1966.

As the title indicates, a focus on the leader as a person.

APPENDIX B

Footnotes

Preface

1. C. Roland Christensen, Norman Berg, and Malcolm S. Salter, *Policy Formulation and Administration*, 8th ed. (Homewood, Ill.: Richard D. Irwin, 1980).

2. Cases written at the Harvard Business School are available through HBS Case Services, Harvard Business School, Soldiers Field, Boston, Mass. 02163. Information on cases written at other schools may be obtained directly from the authors or from the "Directory of Management Cases, Information and Sources, 1983" available from HBS Case Services.

3. Edmund P. Learned, C. Roland Christensen, Kenneth R. Andrews, and William D. Guth, *Business Policy: Text and Cases* (Homewood, Ill.: Richard D. Irwin, 1965). The text portion was written by Professor Andrews. The latest version of that text may be found in Kenneth R. Andrews, *The Concept Corporate Strategy*, rev. ed. (Homewood, Ill.: Richard D. Irwin, 1980) and in C. Roland Christensen, Kenneth R. Andrews, Joseph L. Bower, Richard G. Hamermesh, and Michael E. Porter, *Business Policy: Text and Cases,* 5th ed. (Homewood, Ill.: Richard D. Irwin, 1982).

Chapter 1

1. C. Roland Christensen, "Education for the General Manager," Harvard Business School, Case no. 9-375-241.

2. Kenneth R. Andrews, *The Concept of Corporate Strategy*, rev. ed. (Homewood, Ill.: Richard D. Irwin, 1980).

3. Henry Mintzberg, *The Nature of Managerial Work* (New York: Harper & Row, 1973).

4. John P. Kotter, *The General Managers* (New York: Free Press, 1982).
5. C. Roland Christensen, *Teaching by the Case Method* (Boston: Division of Research, Harvard Business School, 1981).
6. Kenneth R. Andrews, "Letter from the Editor," *Harvard Business Review*, July–August 1981, p. 1.
7. See footnote 2 of Preface.

Chapter 2

1. Michael E. Porter, *Competitive Strategy* (New York: Free Press, 1980).
2. "Polaroid–Kodak," Harvard Business School, Case no. 9-373-266.
3. Alfred P. Sloan, *My Years with General Motors* (New York: Doubleday Publishing, 1964).
4. "The Lincoln Electric Company," Harvard Business School, Case no. 9-376-028.

Chapter 3

1. Theodore Levitt, "The Globalization of Markets," *Harvard Business Review*, May–June 1983.
2. Kenneth R. Andrews, *The Concept of Corporate Strategy*, rev. ed. (Homewood, Ill.: Richard D. Irwin, 1980).
3. John P. Kotter, *The General Managers* (New York: Free Press, 1982).

Chapter 4

1. Lorna M. Daniells, *Business Information Sources* (Berkeley: University of California Press, 1976).
2. Baker Library at the Harvard Business School, for example, lists all publications received in a bibliography entitled "Current Periodical Publications."
3. Michael E. Porter, *Competitive Strategy* (New York: Free Press, 1980).
4. Sidney Schoeffler, Robert D. Buzzell, and Donald F. Heaney, "Impact of Strategic Planning on Profit Performance," *Harvard Business Review*, March–April 1974.
5. Robert D. Buzzell, Bradley T. Gale, and Ralph R. M. Sultan, "Market Share—A Key to Profitability," *Harvard Business Review*, January–February 1975.
6. Carolyn Woo and Arnold Cooper, "The Surprising Case for Low Market Share," *Harvard Business Review*, November–December 1982.
7. Richard G. Hamermesh, M. J. Anderson, Jr., and J. E. Harris, "Strategies for Low Market Share Business," *Harvard Business Review*, May–June 1978.
8. Note on the "Use of Experience Curves in Competitive Decision Making," Harvard Business School, Case no. 9-175-074.
9. William K. Abernathy and Kenneth Wayne, "Limits of the Learning Curve," *Harvard Business Review*, September–October 1974.

Chapter 5

1. Alfred P. Sloan, *My Years with General Motors* (New York: Doubleday Publishing, 1964), chapter 9.
2. Erich Helfert, *Techniques of Financial Analysis* (Homewood, Ill.: Richard D. Irwin, 1982).
3. *Dun's Review*, monthly.

Chapter 6

1. "Polaroid: Turning Away from Land's One-Product Strategy," *Business Week*, March 2, 1981, pp. 108–12.
2. "Midway (D2)," Harvard Business School, Case no. 9-306-138.
3. Chester Barnard, *The Functions of the Executive* (Cambridge, Mass.: Harvard University Press, 1960), p. 224. Reprinted by permission.
4. As reported in *The Wall Street Journal*, October 2, 1978.
5. Thomas Peters and Robert Waterman, Jr., *In Search of Excellence* (New York: Harper & Row, 1982).

Chapter 7

1. Joseph Auerbach, "The Now and Future Business Corporation," Harvard Business School, Working Paper 83-54, 1983.
2. Milton Friedman, "The Social Responsibility of Business Is to Increase Its Profits," *The New York Times Magazine*, September 13, 1970, pp. 32–33, 122, 124, and 126.
3. "Sturm Ruger and Company," Harvard Business School, Case no. 9-375-114.
4. "Florida Becomes Gun Trading Center," *The Boston Globe*, October 11, 1982.
5. Carl Kaysen, "The Corporation: How Much Power? What Scope?" in *The Corporation in Modern Society*, ed. Edward Mason (Cambridge, Mass.: Harvard University Press, 1960).

Chapter 8

1. Chester Barnard, *The Functions of the Executive* (Cambridge, Mass.: Harvard University Press, 1960). Reprinted by permission.
2. "Textron in the Eighties," Harvard Business School, Case no. 1-383-111, p. 11.
3. Joseph L. Bower, *Managing the Resource Allocation Process* (Boston: Division of Research, Harvard Business School, 1970).
4. "The Lincoln Electric Company," Harvard Business School, Case no. 9-376-028, p. 1.

Chapter 9

1. Douglas McGregor, *The Human Side of Enterprise* (New York: McGraw-Hill, 1960).

2. Robert Tannenbaum and Warren H. Schmidt, "How to Choose a Leadership Pattern," *Harvard Business Review*, March–April 1958.

3. Ibid., p. 101.

4. Abraham Zaleznik, "Managers and Leaders: Are They Different?" *Harvard Business Review*, May–June 1977.

5. "The Lincoln Electric Company," Harvard Business School, Case no. 9-376-028, p. 26.

6. Polaroid Corporation 1980 Annual Report, p. 3.

Chapter 10

1. Portions of this chapter have been adapted from a working paper by Philippe C. Haspeslagh and Norman Berg entitled "Diversification and Mergers: Some Trends and Results," Harvard Business School, Working Paper no. 79-2, 1979.

2. Richard P. Rumelt, *Strategy, Structure and Economic Performance* (Boston: Division of Research, Harvard Business School, 1974).

3. Bruce R. Scott, "The Industrial State: Old Myths and New Realities," *Harvard Business Review*, March–April 1973.

4. Alfred D. Chandler, Jr., *Strategy and Structure* (Cambridge, Mass.: MIT Press, 1962).

5. See Malcolm S. Salter and Wolf A. Weinhold, *Diversification Through Acquisition* (New York: Free Press, 1979) for a discussion of major merger waves as well as other aspects of diversification.

6. Stanley Vance, *Managers in the Conglomerate Era* (New York: Wiley-Interscience, 1971).

7. E. Ralph Biggadike, *Corporate Diversification: Entry, Strategy, and Performance* (Boston: Division of Research, Harvard Business School, 1979).

8. Norman D. Fast, *The Rise and Fall of Corporate New Venture Divisions* (Ann Arbor, Mich.: UMI Research Press, 1978).

9. Hapeslagh and Berg, "Diversification"; and Thomas E. Copeland and J. Frederick Weston, *Financial Theory and Corporate Policy* (Reading, Mass.: Addison-Wesley Publishing, 1976), chapters 17 and 18; and United States Senate, *Mergers and Economic Concentration—Parts I and II*, Hearings before the Subcommittee on Antitrust, Monopoly, and Business Rights of the Committee of the Judiciary, March–April 1979.

10. Paul Asquith, Robert F. Bruner, and David W. Mullins, Jr., "The Gains to Bidding Firms from Merger," *Journal of Financial Economics* 11 (1983), pp. 121–39.

11. Richard P. Rumelt, "Diversification Strategy and Profitability," *Strategic Management Journal*, 3 (1982), p. 361. Reprinted by permission of John Wiley & Sons, Ltd.

Chapter 11

1. Alfred D. Chandler, Jr., *Strategy and Structure* (Cambridge, Mass.: MIT Press, 1962).

2. William K. Hall, "SBUs: Hot, New Topic in the Management of Diversification," *Business Horizons*, February 1978.

3. "General Electric—Strategic Position: 1981," Harvard Business School, Case no. 9-381-174.

4. "General Electric—Business Development," Harvard Business School, Case no. 9-382-092; and "The Job of the Chief Executive and Business Development," Harvard Business School, Videotape no. 9-882-024.

5. Norman Berg, "Strategic Planning on Conglomerate Companies," *Harvard Business Review*, May–June 1965.

Chapter 13

1. See, for example, J. Frederick Weston and Eugene F. Brigham, *Managerial Finance*, 6th ed. (Hinsdale, Ill.: Dryden Press, 1978), especially chapter 22.

2. Berkshire Hathaway, Inc., Annual Letters to Shareholders, 1977–1981, p. 40.

3. See, for example, Burton Malkiel, *A Random Walk Down Wall Street* (New York: W. W. Norton, 1975); and David Dremen, *Contrarian Investment Strategy* (New York: Random House, 1979).

Chapter 14

1. For a more detailed explanation of portfolio planning models, see Malcolm S. Salter and Wolf A. Weinhold, *Diversification Through Acquisition* (New York: Free Press, 1979), chapter 4; or Gerald B. Allan, "A Note on the BCG Concept of Competitive Analysis and Corporate Strategy," Harvard Business School, Case no. 9-175-175.

2. Philippe Haspeslagh, "Portfolio Planning: Uses and Limits," *Harvard Business Review*, January–February 1982.

3. William K. Hall, "SBUs: Hot, New Topic in the Management of Diversification," *Business Horizons*, February 1978.

4. Carolyn Woo and Arnold Cooper, "The Surprising Case for Low Market Share," *Harvard Business Review*, November–December 1982.

5. Richard G. Hamermesh, M. J. Anderson, Jr., and J. E. Harris, "Strategies for Low Market Share Business," *Harvard Business Review*, May–June 1978.

Chapter 15

1. Norman Berg, "The Corporate Role in Diversified Companies," Harvard Business School, Working Paper, 1970; and Allan Conway "The Evolution of the Role of the Corporate Office in the Diversified Firm," doctoral thesis, Harvard Business School, 1983.

INDEX

General manager
and the administrative point of view, 8–10
administrative skills needed by, 9–10
authority and responsibility of, 110–13
categories of responsibility, 6–7
and cooperation and competititon, 108–10
effect of rewards on behavior of, 107–8
effect of values of, on organization, 61–63
environment of, 7–8
fairness, respect, and participation, 113
impact of values of on, 64–65
intellectual skills needed by, 9–10
job of, 3–11
as leader, 103–14, 185
leadership styles of, 104–7
nature of job, 5–6
personal guidelines for dealing with strategy, 65–66
personal skills of, and strategy implementation, 89–90
responsibilities of, to constituencies, 4–5
General Motors, 25, 29, 43, 50, 51, 122
Government organizations, general management positions in, 3
Grace, W. R., Company, 45
Grey, Harry, 167
Gulf & Western, 181

H
Hall, William K., 135, 177
Hammermesh, Richard G., 45n, 178n
Hamm's Brewery, 168
Handguns, manufacturer of, and corporate responsibility, 72–74
Harrah's gambling casino, 64–65
Harris, J. E., 45n
Haspeslagh, Philippe, 120n, 129n, 177
Heaney, Donald F., 45n
Helfert, Erich, 54
Heublein, 167, 168
Hewlett-Packard, 36
Holiday Inns, Inc., 64–65
Hostile tender offers/takeovers, 126–27
Human resources, 55–56

I
IBM, 149
Incentives, group versus individual, 110
Industrial organization, field of, 41
Industry
economic characteristics of, 38–40
effect of various factors on, 48–49

Industry—Cont.
identification of present position of company in, 52
importance of environment for, 35–49
makeup of, 35–38
sources of data on, 40–41
Industry dynamics, 41–44
Informal organization, and strategy implementation, 94–95
Information systems, and strategy implementation, 95–97
Ingersoll-Rand, 181
Instant photography industry, 37
Integration, achievement of objectives regarding, 24
Intellectual skills, of general manager, 9–10
Interest rates, effect of high, on industry, 48
IT&T, 96, 181

J
Japanese management
automation and cost efficiency of plants of, 44
cost advantages of manufacturers over American manufacturers, 20–21
and individual versus group incentives, 110
Jaworski, Leon, 78
Jones, Reginald, 137

K
Kaysen, Carl, 85
"Key Business Indicators," 54
Kidde, Walter, 181
Kodak, 37, 43, 153
Koppers, 181
Kotter, John P., 8, 33
Kueffer & Kesser, 36

L
Land, Edwin, 25, 60–61, 116
Leadership styles, 104–7
Learning curves, 46
Leavitt, Theodore, 29
Leisure Group, Inc., 60, 63
Leisure industry, 60
Leveraged buyouts, 163
Lincoln, James F., 113
Lincoln Electric Company, 25, 100
Little, Arthur D., Inc., 174
Little, Royal, 132
Litton Industries, 124, 132, 148, 167, 181
Loft operation, 42
LTV, 124

*This book has been set on Mergenthaler Linotron
202, in 10 point Melior, leaded 2 points. Part numbers and titles are 24 point Melior Semibold Italic.
Chapter numbers are 18 point Melior Semibold
Italic and chapter titles are 24 point Melior Regu-
lar Italic. The size of the type area is 26 by 46½
picas.*